REVISED CUSTOMER SATISFACTION:

The Other Half of Your Job

Dru Scott, Ph.D.

A FIFTY-MINUTE™ SERIES BOOK

CRISP PUBLICATIONS, INC.
Menlo Park, California

REVISED
CUSTOMER SATISFACTION:

The Other Half of Your Job

Dru Scott, Ph.D.
President
Customer Satisfaction Tools

CREDITS
Editor: **Michael G. Crisp**
Designer: **Carol Harris**
Typesetting: **Interface Studio**
Cover Design: **Carol Harris**

Printed in the United States of America

English language Crisp books are distributed worldwide. Our major international distributors include:

CANADA: Reid Publishing, Ltd., Box 69559—109 Thomas St., Oakville, Ontario Canada L6J 7R4. TEL: (416) 842-4428; FAX: (416) 842-9327

AUSTRALIA: Career Builders, P.O. Box 1051, Springwood, Brisbane, Queensland, Australia 4127. TEL: 841-1061, FAX: 841-1580

NEW ZEALAND: Career Builders, P.O. Box 571, Manurewa, Auckland, New Zealand. TEL: 266-5276, FAX: 266-4152

JAPAN: Phoenix Associates Co., Mizuho Bldg. 2-12-2, Kami Osaki, Shinagawa-Ku, Tokyo 141, Japan. TEL: 3-443-7231, FAX: 3-443-7640

Selected Crisp titles are also available in other languages. Contact International Rights Manager Suzanne Kelly at (415) 323-6100 for more information.

Library of Congress Catalog Card Number 88-70488
Scott, Dru
Customer Satisfaction: The Other Half of Your Job
ISBN 1-56052-084-1

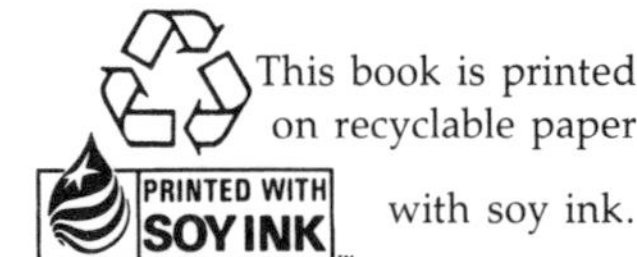

This book is printed on recyclable paper with soy ink.

ABOUT THIS BOOK

CUSTOMER SATISFACTION: THE OTHER HALF OF YOUR JOB is not like most books. It stands out from other books in an important way. It's not a book to read — it's a book to *use*. The unique "self-paced" format of this book and the many exercises encourage a reader to get involved and try some new ideas immediately.

This book introduces you to concepts of why customer satisfaction is important to you and your organization.

This book can be used effectively in a number of ways. Here are some possibilities.

— **Individual Study**. The book is self-instructional. By completing the activities and exercises, a reader should not only receive valuable feedback, but also practical steps for self-improvement.

— **Workshops and Seminars**. The book is ideal for assigned reading prior to a program. With the basics in hand, the quality of participation will improve. The book is also effective when distributed at the beginning of a session, and participants work through the contents.

— **Remote Location Training**. Books can be sent to those not able to attend "home office" training sessions.

There are several other possibilities. One thing for sure, even after it has been read, this book will be looked at — and thought about — again and again.

ABOUT THE AUTHOR

Author, film personality, psychologist, and seminar speaker, Dru Scott is an internationally known authority on customer satisfaction. Dru has been featured in six films, has authored five books with combined sales of two million copies. Her client list includes such organizations as Du Pont, AT&T, American Express, the American Dental Association, and the University of California, among many others.

Dr. Scott is President of the San Francisco based firm of Customer Satisfaction Tools, a company devoted to sustaining quality customer service.

Dedicated to:

JIM ANDERSON

Managing Director, General Services

E. I. DU PONT DE NEMOURS & CO., (INC.)

For his leadership in Quality through serving internal customers

For providing a vital part of the laboratory for the research behind this book

CONTENTS

PART I

GETTING A GOOD START

SECTION ONE

TODAY, MORE THAN EVER, WHY READ THIS BOOK?

Customer service. Customer satisfaction. It seems everyone is talking about customers. Why then, is poor service still a major concern of most organizations? And why are dedicated people still feeling so stressed when involved with customers despite all that has been said and written? Some of the reasons are:

First, few people have been trained to pay attention to the other half of today's jobs — the people part. They have invested their time and energies in the technical aspects. They have not been trained to handle the complications of making sure their work adds value to others.

YESTERDAY
TECHNICAL RESPONSIBILITIES

TODAY	
TECHNICAL RESPONSIBILITIES	PEOPLE RESPONSIBILITIES

Second, people have not been conditioned or encouraged to treat people *inside* of their own organization as well as they treat customers outside. Yet no one works alone. Without the support and cooperation of internal people it is difficult to satisfy those we commonly view as our ''real'' customers (those who buy our products or services). Satisfying internal people provides a vital link in the chain that leads to satisfying customers outside of the organization.

Third, people often don't realize that working hard is not the same as satisfying customers. As a result, people often work hard and are frustrated because customers remain unsatisfied.

CUSTOMER SATISFACTION SKILLS PAY OFF SIX WAYS

YOUR PERSONAL BENEFITS

You benefit from customer satisfaction in three important ways:

1. **LESS STRESS**

Those who deal with customers are often placed in stressful situations. They need to learn to deal with stress constructively in order to maintain a high level of personal satisfaction and service to others. This book will teach you how to reduce your feelings of stress.

2. **GETTING MORE DONE WITH FEWER PEOPLE**

Organizations around the world — in both the private and public sector — are asking fewer people to produce more.

When you concentrate on the customer satisfaction principles in this book you will get a better handle on what customers want and do not want and on what needs to be done and what can be streamlined. You will learn how to trim the unnecessary aspects from your job. You will learn how to get more done with fewer people by focusing on how to promote and encourage cooperation. When you concentrate on customer satisfaction, you have a unifying purpose that leads to better teamwork and improved productivity.

3. **MORE SATISFACTION**

Successful organizations know how to attract and keep productive people. They have learned that there must be opportunities for satisfaction and that work must have meaning.

When you are able to see how your job benefits your customers, your personal satisfaction goes up. You add meaning to your work when you have a clear customer orientation.

YOUR ORGANIZATIONAL BENEFITS

Your organization benefits from customer satisfaction in the following practical ways:

1. KEY TO SURVIVAL AND SUCCESS

Organizations that satisfy customers most effectively earn the right to survival. We see it every day. When an organization becomes self-centered and forgets responsibilities to customers, it will lose business and suffer until the customer once again becomes king or queen.

2. RALLYING POINT FOR MOTIVATED TEAMWORK

Study organizations with high customer satisfaction, and you will find an energized, motivated group of employees and managers. People in these organizations have learned to mobilize toward a purpose *outside* of their work group. The customer is a natural stimulus for needed motivation and teamwork.

3. GETTING THE MOST FOR YOUR MONEY

Organizations with good reputations for cost effectiveness often have a close commitment to their customers. Check the records. They provide services and products that satisfy current customer needs. In the public sector as well as the private sector, organizations recognize that customer satisfaction is the keystone for continued success.

MOTIVATED TEAMWORK

WHY THIS BOOK WORKS WHERE OTHERS HAVE FAILED

''They start at Act Two. That's the problem.'' An energetic customer rep summed it up neatly. It's true. Most books and resources for frontline customer satisfaction representatives and managers falter because they forget Act One issues. This book includes this vital foundation.

The following three statements reveal the often overlooked issues.

1. **''But my situation is different. I don't have customers.''**

   This shows the need for better understanding of customer responsibilities for each individual. An individual (regardless of job title) may not realize that he or she individually has customer responsibilities. Either as a partner with others inside the organization to serve external customers, or as an individual who directly touches the external customer.

2. **''I give good service, they just don't appreciate it.''**

   This shows the need for better understanding of the satisfaction responsibilities for each individual. A person may not have been trained to recognize that customers being satisfied — not just served — is part of his or her job responsibilities.

3. **''I must be doing okay. I haven't had any complaints lately.''**

   This shows the need for more effective customer feedback. Individuals may not receive adequate feedback about when they are — or are not — satisfying customers. Complaints and compliments are not enough. Imagine the difficulty of playing the piano without being able to hear the notes. Or playing a basketball game with no scoreboard. We all do better when we know how we are doing.

Building a solid foundation

As obvious as these three insights can be, more than fifteen years of research, consulting and training in customer satisfaction reveal that they are often neglected. Only after the foundation issues are communicated, will the techniques of dealing with customers be relevant and alive for everyone. Another issue that is often neglected is diversity.

DIVERSITY AND THIS BOOK

RESPECT FOR DIVERSITY FLOWS FROM:

1. The research behind the ideas in this book grows out of work with a rich variety of groups.

2. The ideas and techniques throughout the book will add to your ability to work with individuals representing a wide diversity.

Being of service to varying groups of people

Relating to those with differing backgrounds

Going beyond apparent differences to real connections

Focusing on the core issues that unite and empower

WITH A VISION

Working as partners inside the organization, to benefit customers outside the organization.

THE PATH FORWARD

To help you achieve this vision, you will find the body of the book divided into three parts:

Clearing away barriers and building the foundation

Using the tools

Maintaining customer satisfaction

WHAT YOU WILL LEARN IN THE REST OF THIS BOOK

This book offers skills and techniques you can use to enhance relationships with both internal and external customers. Here's what you will be exploring:

PART I: **GETTING A GOOD START**

PART II: **CLEARING AWAY THE BARRIERS AND BUILDING THE FOUNDATION FOR CUSTOMER SATISFACTION**

Section Two: Shows the best way to handle difficult people inside and outside the organization. The key is to take things professionally, not personally.

Section Three: Discusses the major threat to providing customer satisfaction—job burnout. You will learn eight early-warning signals and five proven ways to keep yourself up and motivated to provide satisfaction every time.

Section Four: Shares the secret of cooperation. Uncovers what happens when you treat each person as a customer.

Section Five: Discusses the difference between customer satisfaction and simply customer service.

PART III: **USING THE TOOLS**

Section Six: Emphasizes the value of problem solving rather than blaming. Provides seven practical steps for handling irate people.

Section Seven: Offers specific words and phrases to build cooperative relationships.

PART IV: **MAINTAINING CUSTOMER SATISFACTION**

Section Eight: Highlights how customer feedback builds motivation, teamwork, and quality and teaches you how to encourage and obtain on-going feedback.

SOME OBJECTIVES FOR YOU

You will be working with more than 50 practical, proven techniques in this book. View them as you would a buffet. Pick the ones that are most beneficial for your work responsibilities, your pressures, your priorities, and the people in your life.

Concentrate on up to five techniques. Selecting more will encourage you to put them aside. Even if you only pick three or four, that's fine. When you pick the right ones for you and concentrate on putting them to work, you reap rich rewards. You reinforce habits that reduce your stress and build job satisfaction.

Fold the corner of this page because it's a useful place to return to as you work through the book. When you discover a technique that would be good for your responsibilities, write it in the space provided below. Then use the list of techniques you select to help you tackle any troublesome areas.

WHAT ARE THE CUSTOMER SATISFACTION TECHNIQUES
YOU WOULD BENEFIT BY USING MORE FREQUENTLY?

1. ____

2. ____

3. ____

4. ____

5. ____

PART II

CLEARING THE BARRIERS AND BUILDING THE FOUNDATION TO CUSTOMER SATISFACTION

SECTION TWO

DEALING WITH DIFFICULT PEOPLE

PREVIEW

No matter what organization you are part of, or what job you are in, sooner or later, you will run into difficult people.

The toughest people to deal with are often not ''outsiders'', but those within your organization.

The best way to work with difficult people is to approach them professionally and not personally.

Being professional means keeping the spotlight on the issue under discussion and away from yourself.

DEALING WITH DIFFICULT PEOPLE

''This job would be great if it weren't for the difficult people.''

If you have echoed the above words at one time or another, you are not alone. The people part of a job is the biggest source of frustration for most people. ''People'' complications surface in a variety of ways.

SEVEN FREQUENT FRUSTRATIONS

Consider your situation. Decide how each of the following seven frustrations relates to your present job. Put an ''X'' on the line to show the level of frequency of the problem in your normal job responsibilities.

1. ***Others blame you for problems over which you have no control.***

   Does not happen ———————————————— Happens frequently

2. ***People pressure you with ''last minute'' requests.***

   Does not happen ———————————————— Happens frequently

3. ***People who do not understand your job make decisions that strongly affect your work.***

   Does not happen ———————————————— Happens frequently

4. ***People don't give you the right information or materials you need to do your job.***

   Does not happen ———————————————— Happens frequently

5. ***People inside the organization do not cooperate with you when you want to serve outside customers.***

   Does not happen ———————————————— Happens frequently

6. ***People change their expectations once a job is underway.***

   Does not happen ———————————————— Happens frequently

7. ***People you depend on do not do their jobs correctly.***

   Does not happen ———————————————— Happens frequently

Chances are you had at least one ''X'' in the far right column. If so, you are like a majority of your colleagues. This book will help you understand these common frustrations and help you deal with them. The next few pages will discuss major job frustrations in more detail.

CHECK FOR FRUSTRATIONS AND CHALLENGES

As you read the following situations, see if you can identify the frustrations and challenges each individual is facing. Place a check ☑ in the box for those which are common for you. Place an ☒ if the situation sounds like someone you know in your organization.

Situation No. 1

> I get frustrated about getting blamed for things I don't control. Others talk to me as though I caused the problem. When I tell them there is nothing I can do, they don't understand. They just get mad. But, there is nothing I can do. I can't lie about it.

Does this feel or sound familiar? ☐

Situation No. 2

> There is no cooperation around here. No wonder we can't meet our due dates. It's people inside our organization that are the problem. They are either late or give me the wrong information. They don't answer their phones. I have to call five times to get an answer, and then it is usually wrong. If the people inside the organization ever get their act together, it would be no problem for me to get my job done.

Does this feel or sound familiar? ☐

Situation No. 3

> The trouble with my job is that people who don't understand what I do are responsible for telling me what to do. This happens not just with our customers, but also with people at the top of our organization. They don't understand how tough it is. Sometimes they don't even know enough to ask for what they want.

Does this feel or sound familiar? ☐

DEALING WITH DIFFICULT PEOPLE (Continued)

If you've been working for more than a few months, you probably can name specific examples that sound like the situations presented on page 11.

Every day, thousands of people in organizations like yours wrestle with these (and similar) frustrations. The examples described on the preceding page are tough. They are often unfair. And yet they are very common. If you encounter any of the seven frustrations listed on page 10, you would probably agree that the people part of the job is the part many employees would like to leave behind.

You are not alone when it comes to people-related problems. Even highly-trained scientists need to get budgets approved and their research accepted by others. Specialized crafts people need others to obtain the necessary materials and/or market their products. Computer specialists find their technical abilities are not enough unless they can deal effectively with people. Analysts face the challenge of communicating complex information to lay people. No one is immune.

Each of us face frustrations and challenges whenever we interact on a regular basis with those ever-so-complicated creatures called people. Although it may often seem so, we probably realize the grass is not greener in another job. Expecting improvement from a new organization or job rarely happens. Blaming your present job bears little fruit. The reality is clear. No matter what organization or job you are in, you eventually will run into difficult people. You might as well develop your skill in dealing with them. The next several pages will assist you.

THE SECRET OF SUCCESS: TAKE IT PROFESSIONALLY AND NOT PERSONALLY

The secret to resolving most ''people problems'' is simple but not easy. It is like being told to ''love your neighbor,'' often easier to say than to do. But, when you learn to separate personal feelings from professional ones, the rewards are high. When you encounter difficult people, this book will teach you how to put this proven secret to work.

Can you think of a situation where you took things personally and not professionally? Perhaps you lost your composure and said things you regretted later. Maybe you felt hurt and mistreated and let your concentration slip. Or you may have become defensive. If any of these sound familiar, take heart, it simply proves you are human.

A PERSONAL CASE

Think about a situation where you took things personally and then describe it in the space provided below:

What were the specifics?

The people? ____

____

What was said? ____

____

What was the setting? ____

____

What was the timing? ____

____

Other factors? ____

____

DEALING WITH DIFFICULT PEOPLE (Continued)

Review the personal situation you described on the previous page. Then determine the possible costs for taking the situation personally. Check any of the following items that apply.

By taking things personally, I felt:

- ☐ guilty
- ☐ like my concentration was interrupted
- ☐ like it hurt a relationship
- ☐ as though it dampened teamwork
- ☐ other ______________________________

Taking things personally can hurt both you *and* others. Taking a situation professionally pays off for everyone.

To help you avoid costly personal situations, learn to listen to yourself. By practicing, you can learn to recognize when you might be starting to take things personally. The list on the next page can help. Make a copy of it and post it in a conspicuous place to remind you to ''listen'' to yourself.

LISTEN FOR THESE SIGNALS

Be on the alert for the following statements. They are your warning light that you may be starting to take things personally.

1. ''How can you soar with eagles when you are cooped up with turkeys?''
2. ''You don't know the people I work with.''
3. ''It's not that easy.''
4. ''Do you know what he/she said!''
5. ''They didn't even . . .''
6. ''I don't have to . . .''
7. ''They never . . .''
8. ''They always . . .''
9. ''No one appreciates me.''
10. ''I don't get paid enough to take things professionally.''

If you ever hear yourself saying any of the above, the answer is clear. You can reduce your stress by learning to take the situation professionally. The following pages will provide practical ways to build your skill in this important area.

SAVE TIME BY TAKING SITUATIONS PROFESSIONALLY

The practical approach of taking things professionally will save you time. You will have fewer pieces to pick up after you calm down. You will learn to think better at challenging moments and increase your chances of doing things right the first time. You will develop better concentration because you do not have nagging thoughts of ''They should have . . .'' or ''I should have . . .'' Allowing your feelings to get in the way interrupts your mind. Learning how to react professionally to the experiences you encounter helps you understand the bigger picture.

A PAID PROFESSIONAL

One savvy respresentative explained how he taught himself to take things professionally when dealing with difficult people. He reminded himself at key moments, "I am being paid to do this job. That means I am a professional. Those with whom I deal don't have to like me. I don't have to like them, but I make my living by handling people professionally and will learn something every time I encounter a difficult situation."

You may find that the people inside of your organization are the toughest to deal with. Even those who know how to handle outside customers with skill and respect, are sometimes totally insensitive to others on the inside.

Whatever the situation, there are ways to identify potential frustrations. The next page will provide one suggestion about how to handle a difficult person.

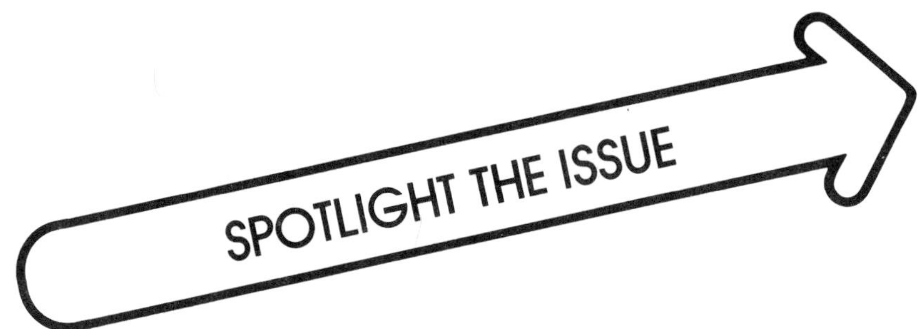

KEEP THE SPOTLIGHT ON THE ISSUE

When you run into a difficult person, give yourself some perspective. Keep the spotlight *away* from yourself and *on* the issue at hand.

TECHNIQUES FOR KEEPING THE SPOTLIGHT ON THE ISSUE

Rather than saying to yourself:	Say instead:
"He is accusing me of making a mistake."	"How can we solve this situation?"
"She can't talk to me like that."	"Will you please tell me what needs to be done?"
"You're not perfect. You make mistakes too."	"This isn't the kind of service we want to provide. What can we do to correct this situation?"

RECAP
SECTION TECHNIQUES

Check the key concepts covered in this section that you agree with.

I agree that:

- ☐ Some of the biggest challenges center on the people part of my job.
- ☐ The toughest people to deal with are often those inside of an organization.
- ☐ The best way to handle both those inside and outside of the organization is to take each situation professionally and not personally.

> FOR REINFORCEMENT
>
> SAY TO YOURSELF:
>
> ''This is my job and I like it. Not because it is easy. Not because there are no difficult people. Not because there are no frustrations. People are a part of any job. I make things easier for myself by taking things professionally.''

Taking things professionally and not personally pays off, but it takes energy and concentration. And it is often a change. When we are faced with the demands and changes of working in today's tight economy, it is easy to let ourselves get into a burnout condition. For these reasons, the next section gives you an easy way to spot burnout. It also gives specific ways of preventing burnout.

SECTION THREE

BURNOUT—THREAT TO CUSTOMER SATISFACTION

PREVIEW

Burnout is a major threat to customer satisfaction. If you allow yourself to burn out, you will not be able to do your best thinking on the job. And you won't have reserves you can call on when you are under periods of high demand.

Read the eight warning signals of burnout presented on page 21 and pinpoint specific signals that apply to you (or your situation). By recognizing potential problems early you will be able to begin working on them before they become difficult to resolve. You may wish to maintain a list of your general and specific warnings signals in some handy place like the inside of your medicine chest.

You can prevent burnout in five powerful ways that will be explained in the pages ahead.

Burnout is common but it is not mandatory.*

* For an excellent book on burnout, order *PREVENTING JOB BURNOUT* by Beverly Potter. See the back of this book.

BURNOUT—THREAT TO CUSTOMER SATISFACTION

"I knew what to do, I just didn't feel like doing it," explained a tall technician about a complaint that erupted late one Thursday afternoon.

This statement pinpoints a symptom of job burnout—knowing what to do, but not getting around to doing it. If you allow yourself to get into a burnout condition, you will not think or act as effectively as you could.

Burnout is a major threat to customer satisfaction because so much of what satisfies customers is positive action based on common sense and job interest. If you are in a burnout condition, you often don't think about positive action steps you could take to satisfy a customer.

Several conditions make burnout particularly dangerous when you work with others. Some examples include:

- When your work focuses mainly on problems or negatives.
- When you rarely hear from people when you are doing a good job.
- When one situation explodes into a problem and a regular customer forgets all of the good work accomplished in previous transactions.

As you read the warning signals on the facing page, think about which apply to you. Also think about which may apply to others with whom you work. Would someone you work with benefit by being more aware of any of the signals listed?

PREVENT JOB BURNOUT

REVIEW THE SIGNALS

To help keep yourself aware of the signals leading to burnout, post the list shown below of *your* burnout indicators on your medicine cabinet (or some other handy place) where you will see it on a regular basis.

Review this list the first of each month. This will help you recognize burnout signals in their early stages. This is the easiest time to get yourself back on track.

EIGHT GENERAL SIGNALS OF BURNOUT

Am I:	YES	NO
1. Communicating less with others?	☐	☐
2. Feeling less energy?	☐	☐
3. Achieving lower productivity?	☐	☐
4. Late for work or appointments more often?	☐	☐
5. Having trouble going to sleep and then waking up at night? Or wanting to sleep all the time?	☐	☐
6. Experiencing unplanned weight loss — or gain? Or eating to eat and not for enjoyment?	☐	☐
7. Preoccupied with my health?	☐	☐
8. Experiencing decreased wants? Showing apathy and a drop in interest in what is happening in the world around me?	☐	☐

PERSONAL SIGNALS OF BURNOUT

In addition to the eight general signals listed on the previous page, there are other specific personal behaviors similar to the following examples. Check any that apply to you.

DECREASED CONCENTRATION ☐

You may find yourself standing by a file drawer. You knew you walked over to get something, but once you are there you can't remember what. Decreased concentration also can be recognized when you become susceptible to interruptions from others and even yourself.

A SHORT FUSE ☐

Little things that you usually take in stride may become major irritants. Traffic may bug you, even when you are in no particular hurry. Or you might snap at a sales clerk who was busy with another customer.

SUSPICION OF JOY ☐

You see someone happy and whistling and think, ''What a phony. It's not normal to feel like that all of the time.''

COMPLAINING ☐

You repeatedly express negative feelings. People around you think, ''Here it comes . . . just like a tape recorder going on and on complaining about the same things again.''

USE OF ARTIFICIAL STIMULANTS ☐

You find yourself taking an extra drink after work, or drinking more coffee or tea, or taking diet pills (or other artificial stimulants). If this begins to happen, it is a major signal to examine what is going on in your life.

DISCOVER YOUR EARLY WARNING SIGNALS

By staying alert it is possible to warn yourself in advance of a potential problem situation. Pinpoint any general or specific signals that you may be on the way to burnout.

FOLLOWING ARE MY PERSONAL SIGNALS OF BURNOUT:

1. ______________________________
2. ______________________________
3. ______________________________
4. ______________________________
5. ______________________________

BURNOUT PREVENTION #1 EXERCISE DAILY

The number one way to prevent (or overcome) burnout wins no popularity contest with those who are feeling run down. Frankly, it is the last thing we want to do when we are feeling frayed around the edges. The best solution however, is physical exercise.

Oxygen is the reason most feelings of burnout disappear after physical exercise. When you exercise, you stimulate the flow of oxygen to your brain. Without ample oxygen, your thinking ability drops. The eight cylinder engine of our mind begins operating on only four cylinders.

If you go home from work feeling tense and drained, even though you do not have a physically demanding job, ask yourself how to beat this feeling. Believe it or not, exercise is the number one way to prevent the feelings of burnout. It is also a vital part of escaping from burnout. Some counselors will not see a client until that person has undertaken an exercise program.

You don't need to run a marathon. Simply walking two miles a day will do it. There are even some ''painless'' alternatives such as watching television as you bounce on a running trampoline, or wearing a ''Walkman'' as you run or walk.

You deserve to feel good. You deserve to think at your best. Create time to exercise regularly. Other burnout tactics will not be as effective until you exercise and stimulate the vital flow of oxygen to your brain on a daily basis.

BURNOUT PREVENTION #2
TAKE CARE OF YOUR OWN NEEDS

Nationally known teacher of behavioral medicine and faculty member of the Louisiana State University Medical Center/Shreveport, Paul D. Ware, M.D., points out the following important considerations so you won't resent being of service to others. He suggests:

Taking care of your own needs and wants:

1 — without devaluing yourself,

2 — without devaluing others,

3 — and, without devaluing the situation.

Devaluing yourself might be an overweight person using a double banana split as a reward.

Devaluing others might be an individual who refuses to answer a co-worker's ringing telephone.

Devaluing the situation might mean goofing off when a person is being paid to work.

Some examples of taking care of your own needs and wants include:

- Making sure your good ideas get attention even if it takes speaking up several times, or putting your ideas in writing.
- Asking people to notice your work accomplishments rather than hoping they will notice.
- Asking directly for what you want, rather than feeling resentful because someone did not provide it without your asking.

BURNOUT PREVENTION #3 WORK TOWARD MEASURABLE TARGETS

Probe into a burnout condition and you'll frequently find a lack of direction and no measurable targets.

Without measurable targets it is difficult to achieve a sense of accomplishment. In too many jobs, workers hear nothing if things are going well. This is a poor situation because most people feel the need to be appreciated.

The realities are that in problem-oriented work, your telephone will never ring off the hook with people calling to express appreciation. The service you provide is expected. There are ways to compensate for this lack of unsolicited positive reinforcement, however. Working with specific targets can help you appreciate the quality of work being accomplished.

TARGETS HELP YOU APPRECIATE YOUR ACCOMPLISHMENTS

Even if no one notices your contribution, you can compliment yourself for meeting meaningful, measurable targets. Here's an example: A woman responsible for writing up job tickets confessed, ''I opposed standards and objectives before we established some targets, but I have changed my mind. They work.'' ''Here's my evidence,'' she added with a smile as she displayed perfectly shaped fingernails. ''I used to chew my nails wondering how I was doing. Now I realize that when I complete at least twelve tickets a day, my supervisor feels I'm doing a good job. I compliment myself. I don't worry if my supervisor hasn't counted them that day. Simply knowing I'm making a contribution has made me feel good about what I do.''

TARGETS TURN ON YOUR CREATIVITY

If you are simply told how to do something and then left alone, it is easy to get bored and lose interest. On the other hand, when *what* you are achieving is explained and you are told *why* it is important, you will feel like you are making a contribution. Once you know the purpose of your job, you are less likely to make mistakes because you know *why* something is being done. Once you understand your role, you are in a position to think of ways to accomplish it even more efficiently by using your creativity.

TARGETS MAKE YOUR JOB EASIER

For many, a few encouraging words about ''Keeping everybody happy,'' is the extent of the customer satisfaction training. This, of course, isn't very helpful. Some people will never be happy no matter what you provide for them. Others will not be happy about anything on a particular day. It is not very realistic to have as the only target a general ''Keep everybody happy.'' Instead, request or give yourself the energizing direction of specific objectives.

SAMPLE TARGETS TO STIMULATE YOUR THINKING

20 service requests completed a day

80 error-free document pages prepared a day

8 recommendations adopted a week

Average daily sales at your station of over $800

20 vouchers audited a day

20 purchase requests placed a day

On-time performance of 100%

Add your own:

____

____

____

____

____

____

____

WORK TOWARD MEASURABLE TARGETS (Continued)

YOU CAN DESIGN YOUR TARGETS

Although targets will help prevent burnout and make jobs more enjoyable, designing them is not always easy. Following is an example of how a creative woman learned to make her job as a server in a conference facility more interesting. ''I make it a game,'' Debbie explained. ''The first day of a two-day seminar, I check on the coffee and danishes several times to make sure there is plenty of each. I want to make sure each group has enough, but not too much. On the second day (based on what the group devoured the first day), my goal is for there to be one danish left over before lunch. If there are no danishes left, someone might have wanted one and it wasn't available. If more than one is left, we have wasted some food.''

While Debbie's target is unique to her job, her creativity is an inspiration. Designing targets for a service responsibility is more challenging than for production or sales jobs. Service is reactive. It is less predictable. But having measurable targets will help anyone, regardless of job, prevent burnout.

You may be thinking, ''But I would feel even more burned out if I had targets and did not meet them.'' This does sound logical. However, there are some surprising results. Knowing where you stand is a powerful burnout prevention factor. Most people want to know specifically where they stand rather than having only a vague notion of how they are doing. Also, targets can always be adjusted up or down as reality dictates.

In the space below describe a target that you either use or could use to make your work more valuable and challenging.

____

____

____

____

____

____

____

____

BURNOUT PREVENTION #4 SAY WHAT YOU FEEL DIRECTLY AND SKILLFULLY

You may be inclined to point out that saying what you feel isn't always easy. It's not. Once you learn how (and when) to do it, however, it is a valuable skill with tremendous benefits. Like any skill, practice will make it easier.

Pick one work situation where you have felt upset, but didn't communicate it to anyone directly. Give the situation a title.

____

Now jot down a few sentences in the space provided describing the situation:

____

____

____

____

____

____

____

____

____

____

You will be asked to return to this situation once you explore some of the complications of communicating directly that are presented in the next few pages.

BURNOUT AND COMPLAINING

AVOID THE TEMPTATION

Have you ever been tempted to tell Person B about a problem situation you are having with Person A? Tempting, isn't it? But, if you tell Person B, you may have noticed that your relief is only temporary. Even though you spent time telling Person B about the problem, normally that individual is not in a position to solve it for you. Chances are Person A may not ever know how frustrating you find the situation with him or her unless you involve them directly.

We do not get a sense of closure when we tell the wrong person. We therefore maintain our urge to tell someone else or to repeat ourselves. Check this out for yourself. Can you think of someone who complained to you about someone else, and then expressed the same complaint over and over? Such a scene is time wasting and very tiring. Also, the problem never seems to get solved. When you say what you feel directly (even if it isn't easy), it will clear the air and you will feel more energized.

Simply being direct is not enough. Your communication needs to be delivered with skill. Blurting out exactly what you feel will normally not serve you or the other person. Neither will an amateurish, "You make me mad." Find the right time. Use the right skills. The next several pages of this book will help you learn how to communicate directly *and* skillfully.

GIVE YOURSELF A HEAD START

Think about the situation you described on page 29. Using the streamlined format listed below will help you practice a response so you will be ready the next time a situation similar to the one you described occurs.

"I feel frustrated about ______________________________
(specific observable event)

____

____

____

______________________________"

"Will you please ______________________________
(specific observable action)

____

____

____

______________________________"

Rehearsing what you will say out loud to yourself helps. So does saying it into a tape recorder. Best of all, if possible, practice your planned response with someone who respects you, but is not directly involved in the situation. Ask for feedback about the reasonableness of your message and your voice tone.

Don't lose momentum. When the situation crops up again, think about what you want to say and then communicate directly with the person involved.

Commit yourself to saying what you feel directly *and* skillfully. Develop your skill through practice. Other people will appreciate it and respect you for it. You will also feel better. Every time you are successful at direct communication, the easier it becomes to do it again. Also you are preventing burnout when you communicate directly.

BURNOUT PREVENTION #5 DO GOOD THINGS FOR YOUR SPIRIT

Learn how to keep yourself positive* and motivated. Discover those things that add energy and a lift to your day. Often they are small acts that you control. They might be as simple as using a favorite pen or pencil, sharing a joke with a co-worker, or having soft music playing in the background.

In the space provided, make a list of your "spirit raisers." You don't have to show this list to anyone, so turn on your creativity.

What are good things you can do for your spirit on company time? Include items that will not disrupt your productivity or distract those around you.

1. ____________________
2. ____________________
3. ____________________
4. ____________________

What are some good things for your spirit that you can do on your own time? Include things that take less than three minutes or that do not cost any money.

1. ____________________
2. ____________________
3. ____________________
4. ____________________

---

*For an excellent book on this subject, order *Attitude: Your Most Priceless Possession* using the information in the back of this book.

RECAP
SECTION TECHNIQUES

Check the techniques you plan to use to prevent job burnout.

I will:

- ☐ Post a note with the eight general signals of burnout plus my specific personal signals.
- ☐ Prevent burnout five powerful ways by:
    - ☐ Exercising daily.
    - ☐ Taking care of my own needs and wants without devaluing myself, others, or the situation.
    - ☐ Defining some measurable personal targets and working to achieve them.
    - ☐ Doing good things for my spirit.
    - ☐ Saying what I feel directfully and skillfully.

FOR REINFORCEMENT

SAY TO YOURSELF:

''Even though burnout is common, it is not mandatory. I take care of myself so that I keep myself up, energetic, and thinking clearly.''

Another good way to reduce the probability of burnout is to encourage cooperation with others in your organization. Take steps to build cooperation, and you will make your job less stressful and more satisfying. The next section pinpoints a powerful way to generate needed cooperation.

SECTION FOUR

THE SECRET TO GETTING MORE COOPERATION

PREVIEW

Cooperation makes a real difference at work. It makes the difficult easier.

Yet we often do not get the cooperation we want because we believe that cooperation is given rather than earned.

The secret to getting more cooperation is to treat each person in your organization as well as you would an important customer.

This approach turns work into satisfying partnerships.

THE SECRET TO GETTING MORE COOPERATION

"There is no cooperation around here."

This indictment echoes across organization after organization. A lack of cooperation in any organization will invite burnout, drain energies, waste time, and lower the quality of the work. On the other hand, working in a place where a spirit of cooperation exists makes the day go better and the work go smoother.

Like apple pie and the flag, everyone is in favor of cooperation. There is no argument with this statement. Why then, don't we have more cooperation at work? The reality is that it is often because of some out-of-date beliefs.

A CLOSE LOOK AT COOPERATION

Let's examine some common beliefs about cooperation.

Please mark "agree" or "disagree" after each statement.

	Agree	Disagree
1. "I can count on people giving me cooperation because it is part of their job."	______	______
2. "I need to do things to earn cooperation."	______	______
3. "Some people are cooperative and others aren't."	______	______
4. "I can do things to increase the probability of each person being cooperative towards me."	______	______

If you agreed with items two and four you understand these are more realistic ways to approach gaining cooperation from others.

COOPERATION IS EARNED MORE FREQUENTLY THAN IT IS GIVEN

A SELFISH AND SUCCESSFUL STRATEGY FOR GETTING MORE COOPERATION

How can you earn better cooperation? Often the people who seem to get the most cooperation are very quiet about their strategy. Yet as you study those who reap the benefits of a rich harvest of cooperation, you will discover the following strategy at work. Those who are most successful have learned to:

FOR COOPERATIVE PARTNERSHIPS

TREAT EACH PERSON AS A CUSTOMER

This strategy simply redirects skills you already use with customers outside of your organization. To get more of what you want, treat each person *inside* of your organization the same as an important external customer would be treated. When you do, you are guaranteed to get more cooperation.

Even though this approach seems like common sense, there are five major barriers which are listed on the next few pages.

ROADBLOCKS TO ADDITIONAL BENEFITS

Roadblock No. 1

"He isn't a customer: He is just someone I work with."

You recognize this attitude if you have ever observed the following. The telephone rings. An individual answers it with an upbeat tone. You can almost hear the musical notes and see the rosebuds. Suddenly there's a change. The person who picked up the phone discovered that the caller is someone inside the organization. The rosebuds disappear. The voice is now a flat and expressionless "Oh, it's you."

No wonder people feel drained at the end of the day. It is hard to feel essential when you hear, "Oh it's you."

Consider another situation. How many times have you wanted to provide service to someone outside of your organization—only to find yourself blocked by someone inside. Needed information is missing. An important telephone call is not returned. A specially requested delivery date was ignored.

You will find you will get more of what you want from people inside of your organization when you learn to treat each one as you would treat an important customer.

Roadblock No. 2

"But you don't know the people I work with."

This is true. No one fully understands the day-to-day demands that you encounter. No one appreciates the creativity and energy you invest to get your work done through people. No other person understands the nuances and complexities of the people you work with.

What we all do understand is this: The more complicated the people aspects of your work, the more interpersonal skills it takes to get what you want. In today's economy, we all experience demands for higher productivity. Many of us are in an unforgiving economic climate with little acceptance of explanations about why a job was not done to expectations.

The more difficult people are to work with, the more **you** benefit by treating each person as a customer.

ROADBLOCKS TO AVOID (Continued)

Roadblock No. 3

"I don't have time."

Treating everyone as you would a customer will actually save you time. This is where the productive selfishness comes in. You probably know someone who talks down to those with less glamorous jobs, such as in the mailroom. "I don't have to treat those turkeys well." Have you noticed how that person's mail often takes longer to arrive than to a person using a more respectful style?

Human nature being what it is suggests that if you treat someone disrespectfully, sooner or later that person will find a way to get even with you. "But I thought you said . . ." "I was only doing what she told me." "Did you see what he did?"

Save yourself the irritation of someone "getting even" sooner or later. It only takes a few seconds more to treat each person as a customer now, and it could save you some nasty surprises in the future.

Roadblock No. 4

"But this approach doesn't always work."

You are right. Nothing in life *always* works. What you need to do is work with the odds. Nothing as complicated as dealing with people can be handled with one technique. Use approaches that have the highest probability of success for you, but always have a handful of Plan B techniques ready in case Plan A does not work.

Roadblock No. 5

"Why should I? I'm the customer."

It is a paradox. Even though you are a customer and deserve respectful and competent treatment, you will get more of what you want if you take the lead. Treat the other person respectfully. Listen. Communicate in ways that make things easier for the other person. Do all the things that a traditional supplier should do. You won't feel guilty afterwards. On the contrary, you will increase the probability of that person wanting to work again with you. Treating someone skillfully pays real dividends. The signals you send out are usually similar to those that are returned.

MORE ROADBLOCKS TO SUCCESS

SIMPLE? "YES." EASY? "NO."

Treat each person as a customer. It sounds simple, but it is not always easy.

Look at the following list of additional roadblocks. Check any you have heard (or perhaps even said):

________ "I'm not good with people. You are either born good with people, or you are not."

________ "It's not my job."

________ "I tried it once. It didn't work."

________ "My situation is different."

________ "No one trained me."

________ "People I work with don't care how it gets done. They just want results."

________ "I know all of this already."

________ "It's not that easy."

(Fill in your own roadblocks)

________ ____

________ ____

________ ____

Which of the above roadblocks might be robbing you of the rewards of smooth-working relationships? Check any that apply. Then when you hear the offending words, recognize them as barriers and take counter-action. It is a good time to turn on your creativity so roadblocks will not stop you from getting the results you want.

FOR COOPERATION AND WORKING AS PARTNERS

To save yourself time

TREAT YOUR BOSS AS YOU WOULD A VALUED CUSTOMER

Although some might say that to treat your boss as a customer is wrong, think of the idea from a different perspective. If you were in the boss's shoes, wouldn't you value being treated with the respect that an important customer receives?

There is an old saying that applies to this situation. ''What goes around, comes around.'' Get more respect and save yourself time, by applying your customer satisfaction skills to your boss.

CASE STUDY
BLAIR AND THE NEW BOSS

Blair's new job was only two months old and she was disappointed already. Her new boss just did not seem to notice her. It seemed like she was always in meetings, and Blair never had a chance to sit down and go over problems with her.

One afternoon as Blair's boss was leaving for a meeting, she stopped by Blair's desk, sat down, and looked her straight in the eyes and said: "Blair, I get the feeling that you think I should go home at night and ask myself, 'How can I make Blair Brownley's job easier?' Well, I don't. What I want you to do is to go home at night and ask yourself, 'How can I make my boss's job easier?' "

For several minutes after Blair's boss left, Blair sat thinking. She was irritated. She didn't like to believe that what her boss said was true, but she knew it was.

The day Blair started treating her boss as an important customer, she started feeling better and getting more of what she wanted.

Blair began to notice that when she asked her boss something, she often didn't get an answer. But when she wrote a note with the same kind of question, sooner or later she always got that note back with an answer written across it. When Blair learned her boss responded better to written inquiries, Blair stopped buttonholing her in the hall with questions. Blair also noticed that her boss used to ask Blair if she had finished things two or three times, even though Blair told her yes. Then Blair decided she would write a brief note for her boss each day describing what had been accomplished.

Now that Blair made her boss's job easier, her boss has begun to single Blair out and tell others what a good job Blair is doing. This positive feedback has helped Blair become a more productive employee who enjoys her job more.

TREAT YOUR BOSS AS A CUSTOMER— SOME QUESTIONS FOR YOU!

Why might some people hesitate to do this?

1. ______________________________

2. ______________________________

3. ______________________________

How can it save you time to treat your boss as you would an important customer?

____

____

What are some other practical reasons to treat your boss as a customer?

____

____

____

____

TREAT CO-WORKERS AS CUSTOMERS TOO!

When you see each person as a customer, you will enjoy more cooperation. You will be using the skills you know to use with people outside the organization in new ways with new advantages to you.

"BUT I DON'T HAVE CUSTOMERS"

PLEASE CHECK EACH STATEMENT EITHER: A for AGREE or D for DISAGREE

	A	D
1. People who talk with those outside of our organization are the only ones who have responsibility for customer satisfaction.	☐	☐
2. "Client" is often a good term to substitute for "customer".	☐	☐
3. People will understand if you are having a down day and are more temperamental than normal.	☐	☐
4. If a person knows how to do something well, they will automatically do it well every time.	☐	☐
5. If something does not feel natural, you automatically shouldn't do it.	☐	☐
6. Your situation may be different, and you don't have customers.	☐	☐
7. If you use a new idea once and it doesn't work, never use it again.	☐	☐
8. Learning customer skills may require the kind of discipline and practice that is common to becoming an accomplished athlete.	☐	☐
9. Every time you pick up the telephone, you *are* your organization.	☐	☐

See author comments on page 112.

RECAP
SECTION TECHNIQUES

To get the most out of this section, check those techniques you plan to use more frequently.

I will:

- ☐ Update my beliefs about cooperation. Cooperation is earned more frequently than it is given.

- ☐ Build cooperative partnerships, by treating each person as a customer both inside *and* outside of my organization.

- ☐ Save myself time by treating my boss as a very important customer.

FOR REINFORCEMENT

SAY TO YOURSELF:

''Even if it is not easy, I treat each person during my workday as a customer. It always pays off. I get better cooperation. And I get the satisfaction of working as a partner.''

As you gain the benefits of treating each person as a customer, it is a natural step to want to refine your ability to handle customers. The next section will explore a subtle but important refinement—moving beyond customer service to customer satisfaction.

SECTION FIVE

THE PROBLEM WITH CUSTOMER SERVICE

PREVIEW

You shortchange both yourself and your customers if you are content to simply provide customer service. To do a superior job it will be necessary for you to go beyond service to customer satisfaction. Customer service is defined by the supplier. Customer satisfaction is defined by the customer.

This important but subtle difference once understood, will build motivation, creativity, and commitment.

By establishing specific targets—and achieving them—you will forge the way for motivated customer satisfaction.

A practical system for negotiating mutually agreed upon targets begins with identifying what you and your customer want and need. Then determine how well you can supply them.

Concentrating on satisfaction and learning how to deliver it, will prevent burnout, build confidence and stimulate more satisfaction for both you and your customers.

THE PROBLEM WITH CUSTOMER SERVICE

"I give good service. The customers just don't appreciate it."

This statement pinpoints the subtle danger of concentrating on customer service alone. Such concentration loses the vital focus of what satisfies the customer— inside or outside the organization.

GO BEYOND SERVICE	AIM FOR CUSTOMER SATISFACTION
Customer service is supplier defined	Customer satisfaction is customer defined

WHY SATISFACTION IS BETTER THAN SERVICE

Think of your response if a waiter walked to your restaurant table and announced, "You had a great dinner!" You would probably smile at such a picture because you are accustomed to a scene where the waiter would ask, "How did you enjoy your dinner?" In this situation, the server lets you decide how satisfied you are, rather than telling you what he thinks.

This scene quickly illustrates the difference between service and customer satisfaction. ***Customer service is provider defined rather than customer defined, where customer satisfaction must always be defined by the customer.***

Don't stop at customer service. Go beyond service to customer satisfaction.

CASE STUDY
TOM AND THE TWO-HOUR TROUBLE

It does make a difference.

If you had asked Tom, a maintenance technician, six months ago if he provided good service, he would have given you a quick ''yes.'' He *did* give good service. He concentrated on doing his job well. He enjoyed being a technician, and took pride in being technically perfect.

But when Tom began to learn about customer satisfaction, he made a change. He used to say that a certain type repair in two hours was ''doggone good service.'' Now he is more sensitive to what his customer thinks is ''doggone good service.'' By asking them, he learned that some expect a progress report every 30 minutes. Others simply want to know when the repair is completed.

When Tom learned to concentrate on customer satisfaction, he found it made a positive difference which showed up in the number of compliments he received. Tom still provides excellent customer service but spends time with each of his clients to insure there is customer satisfaction as well.

MEET THE REQUIREMENTS OF THE PEOPLE YOU SERVE

Assume that you are eating lunch when a co-worker from another group sits down next to you. Before you have taken your first bite, you start to hear a barrage. ''Do you know what happened? This morning someone had the nerve to complain about some work I did for him. I know my job. I've been in it for years. I do good work. What does he know. I'm the expert.''

- What would you say to this person?

- Why might someone believe that they define the value of their work rather than the customer defining the value?

- What techniques could your co-worker use to take criticism professionally and not personally?

- What are three personal advantages for you to find out and satisfy your customer's requirements?

CUSTOMER SATISFACTION IS EASIER WHEN YOU HAVE CUSTOMER SATISFACTION TARGETS

If you are tempted to say that your situation is different and specific targets are difficult to define for your job or don't have a value, consider a different perspective. Teenagers who may have difficulty staying motivated in their studies often can concentrate for hours on a video game. The secret is that these games have specific targets where players can continually measure how they are doing. They receive frequent feedback about how well their objective is being met. Video games are only one example. The reason that bowling, golf, baseball and other sports attract us is because they all have targets and ways of ''keeping score.''

TARGETS BY ANY NAME

Organizations also ''keep score.''* They use different terms to describe their desired results but the purpose is to determine how they are doing. Are you aware of targets in your daily work? Do any of the following names sound familiar? Check those that apply to your situation:

- ☐ Requirements
- ☐ Expectations
- ☐ Goals
- ☐ Objectives
- ☐ ______________________________
  (Other)

The meanings of the terms listed above are not always the same. Check with your manager to make sure you have the precise definition of any term used to measure your accomplishments. Working toward targets by any name will make your job easier and more satisfying.

---

*For two excellent books on ''Keeping Score,'' order *EFFECTIVE PERFORMANCE APPRAISALS* by Robert Maddux and *PERSONAL PERFORMANCE CONTRACTS* by Roger Fritz, using the information in the back of this book.

WHO ESTABLISHES YOUR TARGETS?

Think about your situation. Check the box in front of the statement that best describes your targets, goals or objectives:

- ☐ You provide your targets.
- ☐ Targets are established by your manager.
- ☐ Targets are determined by input from both you and your manager.
- ☐ Targets include customer input as well as input from both you and your manager.

Which statement box do you think will lead to customer satisfaction? Write why you feel this way in the space provided below:

____

____

____

____

____

____

____

____

____

____

____

____

____

WHEN THE TARGET IS PROVIDED BY YOUR MANAGER

The following advice will help you get more satisfaction if your manager has been responsible for providing your customer service targets.

MAKE SURE YOU KNOW THE PURPOSE BEHIND THE TARGET!

Once you fully understand the target you will be able to explain problems that may be unique to your customers. If you do this effectively, you will have less stress and be in a position to speak for your organization. It sometimes takes asking questions of others, but it is worth it. Ask enough questions of customers and co-workers and then share what you have learned with your manager. This will help both of you understand and define the customer service targets that are part of your job.

WHEN YOU HELP DEFINE THE TARGET

Work will be much easier once people, (including those inside of your organization and in your personal life), can articulate specifically what they expect and what would satisfy them. Some do not know what they want or need. Others hope you will guess their needs without them having to tell you. (This is particularly true in personal relationships.) Consider how illogical this statement is: ''If you have to tell people what you want, it doesn't really count.'' It is up to you to help others define their expectations.

There may be some additional complications to finding out specifically what people expect and require. For example:

— You may know more about your specialty than the other person. They may not know enough to be able to ask for what they want.

— You may be working in a rapidly-changing environment and expectations have not been clearly spelled out for anyone.

— You may be simply one person in a chain of dozens handling a service or product and may never even see or talk with the end user.

Although it is not always easy to define the specific expectations and requirements, it is worth the effort to discover as much as you can and communicate your findings with others who are involved.

USE THIS PRACTICAL SHORT CUT FOR DEFINING TARGETS

Keep the diagram presented below in mind as you listen and ask questions.

A great place to start is to determine what the customer wants and does not want—and what your organization wants and does not want and then align these elements. (Many people start with what they do not want. Use this to uncover what they do want.)

START WITH THE FOUR CORNERS
THEN DETERMINE THE TARGET

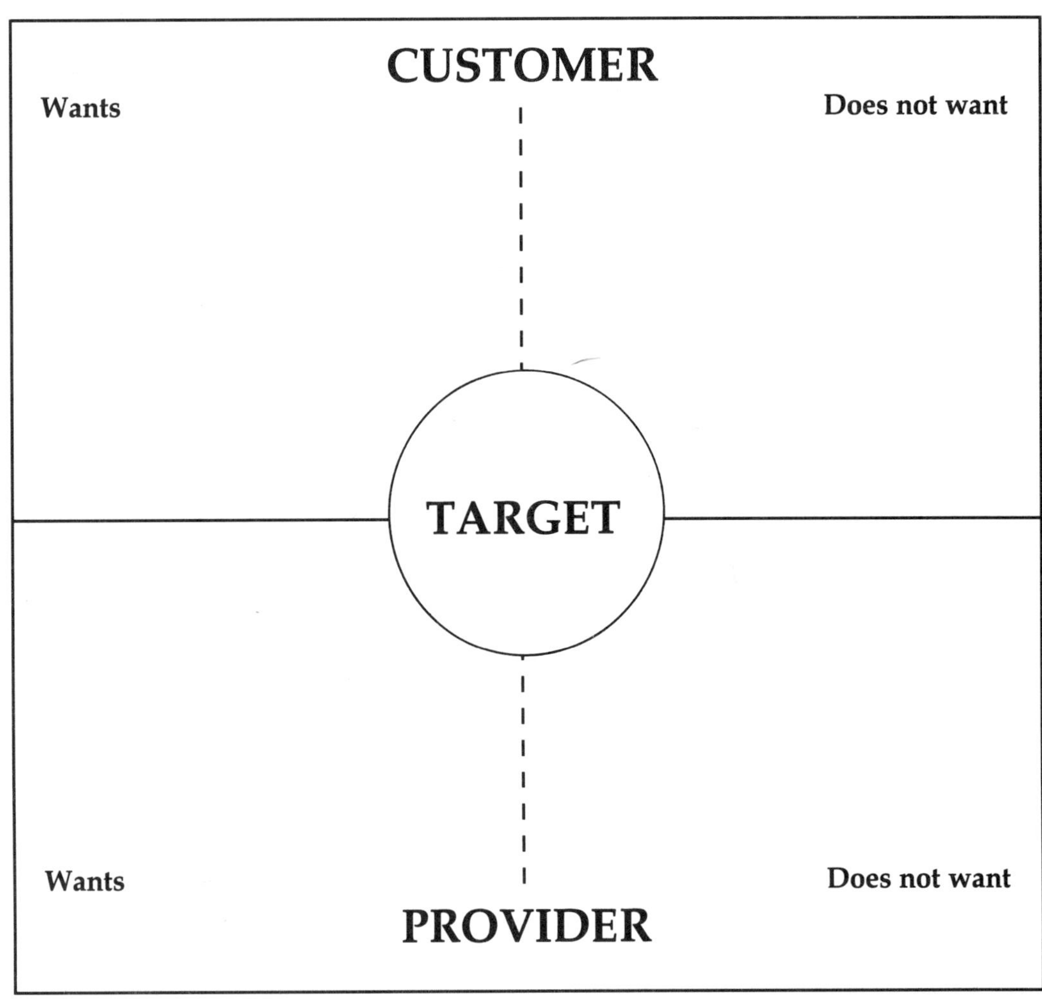

ARM YOURSELF WITH WRITTEN TARGETS

Even though writing out specific targets, expectations or requirements may seem cumbersome, it is a surprisingly strong timesaver. When starting a new project at work, it's easy to nod in agreement that you understand what the target is. This is usually an optimistic conclusion based on the excitement of starting something new. How many times have you been on a committee where someone wrote a summary following the group discussion, then later when it was circulated, the response was *"That's not what I said."* or *"That's not what I wanted."*

Think about your personal life. How many times have you hinted to someone about something you wanted only to have your friend or spouse miss the hint entirely.

In organizations, putting expectations in writing makes sure you and the other person have the best possible understanding of the outcome you both want. By encouraging feedback you prevent misunderstandings later on.

Write some major specific targets which relate to customer satisfaction in your organization.

___

___

___

___

___

___

___

___

___

___

PREPARE TO BE SURPRISED

At first, it may seem time consuming to generate written expectations. It may well slow things at the beginning. But you will be pleasantly surprised how written targets and expectations will pay off. Written targets will prevent rework. They will also prevent the frustration of your not knowing the purpose of what you need to do. Your personal satisfaction will increase because you have a better handle on what your customer wants. You will also reduce the possibility of feeling resentful because you do not get what you want.

AIM FOR SATISFACTION

Answer each of the following questions by circling each statement ''Agree'' or ''Disagree.'' If possible, discuss your responses with your manager.

1.	There are some people you just cannot please.	Agree Disagree
2.	Once you are experienced in working with customers, you automatically know what they want without having to check.	Agree Disagree
3.	Customers are always satisfied when you do a good job.	Agree Disagree
4.	You feel less stress when you understand customer expectations.	Agree Disagree
5.	You feel less stress when you check with customers to see how satisfied they are.	Agree Disagree
6.	All employees are entitled to know how well they are satisfying customers.	Agree Disagree
7.	You waste less time and effort when you know specifically what the expectations of the customer are.	Agree Disagree
8.	Customer feedback always helps make your job better in the long term.	Agree Disagree
9.	Satisfying expectations is the key to meaningful relationships.	Agree Disagree

See author comments on page 112.

RECAP
SECTION TECHNIQUES

To get the most out of this section, check the concepts you plan to use more frequently.

I will:

- ☐ Aim for customer satisfaction rather than merely customer service.
- ☐ Focus my work by using customer-centered targets.
- ☐ Understand the purpose of my customer-centered targets, regardless of how they are assigned.
- ☐ Make sure I can clearly explain all customer-centered targets.
- ☐ Work with my customer to define any vaguely-defined targets.
- ☐ Avoid unnecessary rework by making sure I have a specific direction based on written objectives whenever possible.

FOR REINFORCEMENT

SAY TO YOURSELF:

''Because I do not want to waste my time, I ask questions and listen to learn exactly what others expect from me. They appreciate it, and it makes my job easier.''

Aiming for customer satisfaction, more than simply customer service, does make a difference in how you see people. It also makes it easier to tackle the topic of the next section which explores the technique of solving problems without blaming.

PART III

USING THE TOOLS

SECTION SIX

THE CUSTOMER IS NOT ALWAYS RIGHT, BUT . . .

PREVIEW

THE VALUE OF PROBLEM SOLVING

It's true. The customer is not always right, but it is also true: ***The customer is always the customer.*** This saying means simply that solving the problem is often more important than who is "right". When someone is irritated, if you can solve the problem without blaming yourself or others, you will reduce stress, everyone will feel better, and you will save time. You will be on your way to customer satisfaction.

STEPS TO PROBLEM SOLVING

You will be able to add to your problem solving skills by using seven practical steps presented later in this section. These are guaranteed to assist you in dealing with someone who is irritated.

THE CUSTOMER IS NOT ALWAYS RIGHT, BUT...

"I need this advice the most with people inside of our organization," a pressured technician confided as she pointed to a saying posted to the side of her computer terminal.

The customer is not always right, but the customer is always the customer.

The person who invented this saying deserves a vote of thanks from everyone who works with customers. Considerable time is saved when you learn to not get embroiled in a dialogue with yourself about whether a customer is right or wrong. It doesn't matter if the customer is right or wrong. What matters is that you are committed to providing your customer, whenever possible, with what he or she wants and needs. It is the relationship that matters. Not who is right.

TO HANDLE AN IRATE PERSON

SOLVE THE PROBLEM WITHOUT BLAMING YOURSELF OR OTHERS

BLAMING AS A BARRIER TO PROBLEM SOLVING

> *"That's not my job."*
>
> *"Nobody told me to . . ."*
>
> *"That happened when I wasn't here."*

You've heard these blaming statements enough to recognize what a waste of time they are. Have you noticed that after a person has vigorously blamed someone else, he or she ends up doing the job anyway. But now, that person has not only created a negative impression on the person to whom the statement was made, but also valuable time has been wasted that could have been used solving the problem.

Blaming can also be turned inward. You may be someone who does not blame others, but treats yourself in ways that you would never treat someone else.

> *"You dummy, you should have . . ."*
>
> *"Why didn't you . . ."*
>
> *"You messed it up again."*

Blaming yourself or blaming others are both unproductive. Blaming others wastes time and hurts relationships. Blaming yourself drains energy and often leads to procrastination. Solving problems without blaming is the remedy for both.

BELIEFS AS A BARRIER TO PROBLEM SOLVING

Differing beliefs about problem solving can complicate our lives. We don't usually express the beliefs directly. We only show the edges. The following statements were designed to stimulate your thinking about the beliefs which may be a barrier to problem solving.

UNCOVER YOUR BELIEFS ABOUT PROBLEM SOLVING

Please circle each statement either: A for Agree
D for Disagree

1.	If you did not cause the problem you cannot be hurt by it.	A	D
2.	If you can identify who caused the problem, you are excused from taking action to solve the problem.	A	D
3.	If you did not cause the problem, it is inappropriate for you to help solve it.	A	D
4.	If someone did not tell you what to do, you cannot be responsible for not doing it.	A	D
5.	If you don't understand something, it is the other person's responsibility to make sure that you understand it.	A	D
6.	If you don't understand something, it is your responsibility to make sure you do.	A	D
7.	If the situation is unfair, you are not responsible for doing things to improve it.	A	D
8.	It is reasonable to expect that you will not be given a job until all customer expectations have been completely thought out.	A	D
9.	Defining work expectations and requirements is part of each person's job.	A	D
10.	If someone else makes the mistake, that means you are not responsible for doing anything.	A	D

Discussing your answers with someone else will stimulate your thinking even further. Also, please read the author's recommended responses on page 112 of this book.

SHORTCUT TO STOPPING THE BLAME HABIT—DON'T BE A VICTIM

Although there are a number of beliefs that lead to blaming, one strategy cures them all. It is to solve the problem and skip the blame.

You will be even further ahead when you prevent problems. When you prevent or solve problems, you stay away from the depressing habit of feeling like a victim. People who feel like victims often blame others and themselves. For example: *''No one told me to do that.''* and *''I should have known.''*

The case study on the facing page shows how one person stopped blaming herself and feeling like a victim when she learned how to solve and prevent problems.

CASE STUDY SANDY STEPS OUT OF THE VICTIM ROLE

Sandy related the following situation and the personal benefits she realized.

''Well, my life has certainly changed! Maybe I should say that I changed my life.

''For the first year I was in a specialized order entry job, I was always stressed and running behind. A person would call in with a request at the last minute. I would drop everything and get busy on that request. And then somebody else would call in and request something else. Some days were quiet, but other days it seemed like everyone called. For a long time I complained about other people not being organized. I convinced myself they shouldn't call at the last minute. They should be more understanding.

''Finally, I got tired of feeling like my back was always against the wall. I mentally assumed that people would call at the last minute. My strategy was to change what I was doing. I went through the records and put together a history for several of the ''last minute'' requesters. After I isolated the buying history, I learned to predict with some accuracy when a person would order. I discovered some people called most frequently just before the 15th or the end of the month. Another always called on Friday afternoon. Once I figured out the pattern, I began calling them first. The 12th and 28th of each month gave me more lead time with those who ordered in mid-month or at the end of a month. Calling on Thursday afternoon helped with the Friday-afternoon caller.

''Basically, I stopped waiting for other people to change. I took action to make my situation better, and I feel great! Because I feel in more control, I have less stress.''

Solving problems without blaming yourself or others means less stress, more time, and more satisfaction. You can enjoy even more of these benefits by using the seven steps outlined on the next page.

SEVEN PRACTICAL STEPS TO CUSTOMER PROBLEM SOLVING

Use the following seven steps to calm a person and get a solution under way. This section will show you practical ways to put these steps to work for you. You can use them in order or pick the steps that relate the most to your situation.

STEP 1. **Express respect.**
(Example: "What you're telling me is important.")

STEP 2. **Listen to understand.**
(Example: "Tell me what happened.")

STEP 3. **Uncover the expectations.**
(Example: "Will you please tell me what you feel needs to be done?")

STEP 4. **Repeat the specifics.**
(Example: "Let me make sure I understand what you need . . .")

STEP 5. **Outline the solution or alternatives.**
(Example: "I will take this action." or "You have several choices . . .")

STEP 6. **Take action and follow through.**
(Example: "Your refund has been requested. I will personally check with Accounting to insure your check goes out Friday.")

STEP 7. **Double check for satisfaction.**
(Example: "I'm following up to make sure your check arrived.")

EXPRESS RESPECT

STEP ONE

When people are irritated, it is usually triggered by feeling that their worth has not been recognized. Not recognizing someone's worth is often conveyed unintentionally.

Think about the following situation for a moment. Picture yourself walking into a department store. You know exactly what you want. You get the merchandise and walk to the cash register area, ready to pay. Two sales people are talking. Neither turns to recognize you. Instead, they continue discussing a party they both attended last weekend. What are your feelings as you stand unattended? Chances are you are irritated. You may even put down the merchandise and go to another store. All because people did not bother to communicate your worth as a customer.

Expressing respect for a person and his or her situation will save you time *and* frustration.

When you are confronted with an irritated person, the best thing you can do is to quickly communicate respect. It is almost impossible for someone to be angry with you once you have expressed respect.

EXAMPLES TO STIMULATE YOUR THINKING: EXPRESS RESPECT

No single way of expressing respect works every time or with every person. Because of this, you should have five or six examples of calming language available for use at challenging moments. You may select your favorites from the list shown on pages 66 and 67, or you may develop your own. Experience is the best way to learn which work best with your customers.

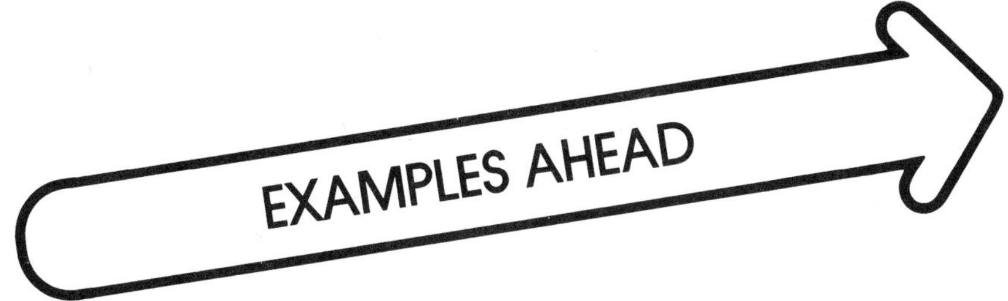

SAMPLES OF CALMING LANGUAGE EXPRESS RESPECT

As you read the following time-saving examples, imagine how you would feel if they were said to you. Give each statement an "X" on a scale of one to ten. A one means you would be irritated, and a ten means such a statement would be calming for you.

1. I will . . . (1 second plus)

   1 2 3 4 5 6 7 8 9 10

   Irritating Calming

2. I will check into this right now. (2 seconds)

   1 2 3 4 5 6 7 8 9 10

   Irritating Calming

3. This is important. (1 second plus)

   1 2 3 4 5 6 7 8 9 10

   Irritating Calming

4. This isn't the kind of service we want to give you. (3 seconds)

   1 2 3 4 5 6 7 8 9 10

   Irritating Calming

5. I apologize. (1 second)

   1 2 3 4 5 6 7 8 9 10

   Irritating Calming

6. Thank you for letting me know about . . . (2 seconds plus)

   1 2 3 4 5 6 7 8 9 10

   Irritating Calming

7. Your work is important to us. (2 seconds)

   1 2 3 4 5 6 7 8 9 10

   Irritating Calming

8. Thank you for telling me about this. (2 seconds)

   1 2 3 4 5 6 7 8 9 10

   Irritating Calming

SAMPLES (Continued)

9. We want you to be pleased with our work. (2 seconds)

1 2 3 4 5 6 7 8 9 10

Irritating — Calming

10. Thank you for your patience. (2 seconds)

1 2 3 4 5 6 7 8 9 10

Irritating — Calming

11. Let me make some notes about what needs to be corrected. (3 seconds)

1 2 3 4 5 6 7 8 9 10

Irritating — Calming

12. I apologize for the inconvenience you have endured. (3 seconds)

1 2 3 4 5 6 7 8 9 10

Irritating — Calming

13. I want to serve you. (2 seconds)

1 2 3 4 5 6 7 8 9 10

Irritating — Calming

Select Your Own Calming Statements

Which examples of calming language could you use? Pick those that fit your situation and the people you work with.

1. ____
   ____
2. ____
   ____
3. ____
   ____

GEORGE

George was heard to say to a co-worker:

> *"If my manager thinks I'm going to tell someone,*
> *'I want to serve you.' then she is mistaken.*
> *I'm not people's servant, especially if they made the mistake.*
> *I am here to help them, but I'm certainly not*
> *here to serve them."*

QUESTIONS FOR DISCUSSION

1. If someone expressed this, how would you predict that person feels at the end of a work day?

2. How satisfied do you think such an individual feels about work?

3. How would you rate this individual's likelihood of experiencing burnout?

LISTEN TO UNDERSTAND **STEP TWO**

Have you ever been irritated and started to explain your situation to someone who doesn't listen? If so, you know how frustrating it can be. For customer satisfaction it is essential to listen for understanding. Listening also provides time to collect your thoughts.

Listen for these vital areas in addition to what the person is saying.

Listen for:

What the person is feeling.

What the person is wanting.

What the person is thinking.

Have you ever confronted someone who is angry, given them the exact answer they wanted, and still had them repeat the original issue? People often do not listen well when they are irritated. You can count on it. People do not listen well when they are angry. What will open the door to improved listening on their part is by your letting them know you understand how they feel. This useful skill is covered in helpful detail in Leadership Effectiveness Training seminars and books. For more information, contact Effectiveness Training, 531 Stevens Avenue, Solana Beach, California 92075.

Listening to understand what people are wanting helps you understand what problem to solve. For example, one person might be irritated about the quality and another about the timing.

Listening for what they are thinking often reveals why they feel the way they do.

''I thought the material was going to be ready by noon today.''

''I knew you would mess up on this again, just like last time!''

''I had no idea it was going to cost this much.''

''I am going to an important meeting and you don't have my materials ready.''

''The way I do my job doesn't count for much anyway.''

**For an excellent self-study book on listening order THE BUSINESS OF LISTENING* by Diane Bone using the information in the back of this book.

CASE STUDY THE BENEFITS OF LISTENING TO UNDERSTAND

Tom told a co-worker:

''I had heard about 'listening to understand' for years. But last Tuesday I decided to do it with every person with whom I came in contact. I was very pleased with the results.

''One customer who regularly calls has always bothered me because she is so abrupt and impatient even when I tried to be friendly. On that Tuesday we had a pause while waiting for some information and we started talking personally. She mentioned that she was tired because she had been wakened at four a.m. by her mother who was suffering from Alzheimer's Disease. Her mother was trying to get dressed and was putting a sweater on her legs like pants. My caller confessed how hard things had become because of her mother's disease.

''My impatience vanished. I began to understand why my caller was often irritable. It had nothing to do with me. It had to do with her family situation.

''I am going to practice listening to understand and try to get to know my customers better. I'm convinced it will make my job more satisfying.''

UNCOVER THE SPECIFIC EXPECTATIONS

STEP THREE

Careful, thoughtful listening will give you a good start toward understanding expectations.

The following examples can assist you in developing your own ways of digging into what the person actually wants and needs. Check those which you can use in your job:

☐ *''Please tell me what needs to be done.''*

☐ *''How can we resolve this situation?''*

☐ *''What can we do right away to get this situation straightened out?''*

☐ *''Was there anything else that wasn't the way you wanted it?''*

☐ *''How can I assist you?''*

Add other examples you can use:

☐ ______________________________

☐ ______________________________

☐ ______________________________

☐ ______________________________

☐ ______________________________

☐ ______________________________

☐ ______________________________

☐ ______________________________

REPEAT THE SPECIFICS

STEP FOUR

You benefit in two ways by repeating your understanding of a customer's expectations. You benefit because:

1. You find out whether or not you understand exactly what the person wants.

2. People calm down once they realize you understand what they want.

Two popular, but ineffective attempts to verify expectations are, "I know" or "I understand." This often inflames rather than calms. The reason is because we do not believe anyone can know (or understand) our exact situation.

Rather than saying, "I know," repeat the specifics in the form of a question. This verification gives evidence of understanding. Aim to have the other person say, "Yes, that's it. You understand."

Here are some examples:

"To make sure I am on the right track, let me double check what you want."

"To prevent a problem, let me summarize what needs to happen."

"So the problem is . . ."

OUTLINE THE SOLUTION OR ALTERNATIVES

STEP FIVE

Handling an irate person is easy when you can solve the problem. If you can, say so immediately.

The tough part is when you cannot give people exactly what they want. In this situation, outline the alternatives. Following are some examples of what you can say:

> *"I will check into this right now, and will get back to you before twelve."*
>
> *"Here is a possibility."*
>
> *"You can . . ."*
>
> *"We do have . . ."*
>
> *"There is an alternative."*

If someone is irate, always have an alternative prepared. This will show your sincere interest in resolving the situation. Saying, "There is nothing I can do," will set some people into an attack mode.

Following are some examples of alternatives when you want to express care even though a solution is unlikely.

> *"I will put a note on my calendar for Friday, and will check again for you."*
>
> *"Sometimes our regional center has what you're looking for. I'll give them a call."*
>
> *"I will put your name on our waiting list in case something develops. In the meantime, I'll keep my eyes open for a possible replacement."*

TAKE ACTION AND FOLLOW THROUGH

STEP SIX

All the benefits discussed in the first five steps will be for naught if you do not take action and then follow through on your commitments. Follow-through occurs in two basic categories: immediate and later. We have all heard the saying ''Do it now.'' This is the best style for immediate resolution. In many instances, however, it is not possible to follow through immediately. Time is required. You may have more than one item to resolve.

YOUR MAJOR WEAPON TO RESOLVE PROBLEMS BY TIMELY FOLLOW-THROUGH IS YOUR CALENDAR OR YOUR WRIST ALARM.

If you tell a person you will get back to him or her before twelve o'clock, do it! If you tell someone you will call before four o'clock on Thursday, make a note in your calendar and do it.

If you have a wrist watch with a built-in alarm, it can be helpful to set it just prior to the time action was promised to insure you have a professional follow-through.

Regardless of which method you choose, make a habit of following through!

DOUBLE CHECK FOR SATISFACTION

STEP SEVEN

Double checking (i.e. following up) for satisfaction is such an essential step an entire chapter is devoted to it later in this book. This part of the book highlights why double checking for satisfaction builds appreciation and loyalty. It is one of the secrets of customer satisfaction.

SOLVING PROBLEMS AND SELF-PROTECTION

The major reason to solve customer problems is for self-protection. This is particularly true when you deal with someone who is irritated. Helping solve their problem will save you time, reduce your stress and make you feel better. Even if you are not to blame for the problem and even if you don't have total control over the outcome, your best bet is still to help get the problem resolved.

RECAP
SECTION TECHNIQUES

To get the most out of this section, check the techniques you will benefit by using more frequently.

I will:

- ☐ Handle an irate person by solving the problem without blaming myself or others.
- ☐ Update any personal beliefs that are barriers to problem-solving.
- ☐ Avoid feeling like a victim.
- ☐ Take the following steps to calm a person and get a solution under way:
    - ☐ Express respect.
    - ☐ Listen to understand.
    - ☐ Uncover expectations.
    - ☐ Repeat specifics to verify that I understand what is expected.
    - ☐ Outline the solution or present alternatives.
    - ☐ Take action and follow through.
    - ☐ Double check for satisfaction.

FOR REINFORCEMENT

SAY TO YOURSELF:

''I solve problems without blaming myself or others. It saves everyone time. It reduces stress, and it builds teamwork. It is particularly practical when handling an irate person.''

Approaching problems in this positive way takes practice. The approach is not automatic, but it is rewarding. The customer satisfaction techniques in the next section are also well worth practicing. They will help you smooth out even the most challenging customer situations.

SECTION SEVEN

GETTING WHAT YOU WANT

PREVIEW

You will get what you want and also get more cooperation when you use the following techniques 100% of the time. They work. And you can use them with people both inside and outside of your organization. They also have an extra benefit. You can adapt each of the following seven techniques to your personal life.

Make it easy for people to cooperate with you.

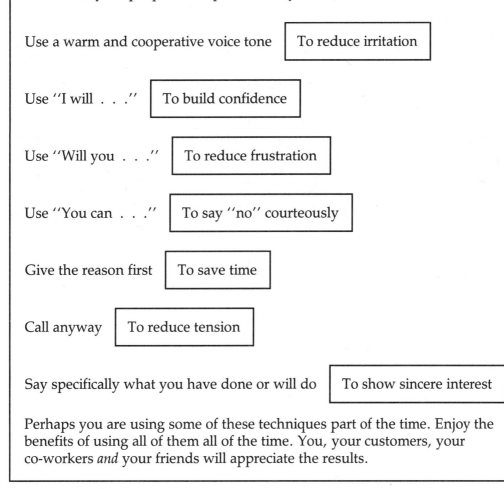

Use a warm and cooperative voice tone — To reduce irritation

Use "I will . . ." — To build confidence

Use "Will you . . ." — To reduce frustration

Use "You can . . ." — To say "no" courteously

Give the reason first — To save time

Call anyway — To reduce tension

Say specifically what you have done or will do — To show sincere interest

Perhaps you are using some of these techniques part of the time. Enjoy the benefits of using all of them all of the time. You, your customers, your co-workers *and* your friends will appreciate the results.

MAKE IT EASY FOR OTHERS TO COOPERATE WITH YOU

> *''I tried it once and it didn't work. Besides, my situation is different.''*

You have probably heard this comment a number of times. It's sad to hear. The belief that one attempt is enough, or that a situation is ''different'' robs people of not only personal satisfaction, but also costs organizations thousands of dollars each year.

Here's why. Excellence grows out of skillful practice. As you watch Olympic competitors on television, you often hear how each individual has practiced thousands of hours in order to compete for only a few seconds or minutes.

As driver of an automobile, you have practiced changing lanes, stopping, and parking hundreds of times. Practice is how you master anything that you do well.

The belief that ''my situation is different'' often diverts people from working on a solution. It is true that each situation is unique, yet there are usually strong similarities to previous incidents. What the ''my situation is different'' belief represents is a lack of flexibility. No one has told that person who makes that statement that almost everything needs to be tailored. If someone goes into a store to buy a jacket, chances are the sleeves need to be changed, some part taken in, another part shortened. It's the same with most customer service situations.

Even though there are differences in situations you face, you can always tailor problem-solving techniques to fit your personality, your pressures, and your customers.

Enjoy even more cooperation by using the researched and proven techniques presented in this section. You, coworkers and customers will benefit.

COOPERATION TECHNIQUE #1

USE A WARM AND COOPERATIVE TONE OF VOICE

Have you ever called someone and had them say all the right words, but still felt they were irritated with you? If so, there's probably an edge in the person's tone of voice.

With practice it is possible to remove irritation from your voice. The following exercises will help:

DEEP BREATHING

If you find your voice (or delivery) is turning people away and slowing you down, lean back and take 60 seconds to breathe deeply. As you relax, breathe in very slowly. Hold your breath for a few seconds. Then breathe out slowly, slowly. Repeat for 60 seconds. This is an emergency treatment for your voice tone. You can get more specifics in *The Telephone and Time Management* by the author of this book. For more information, use the order information in the back of this book.

EXERCISE VIGOROUSLY

Carving out time for vigorous exercise also pays off. You not only sound better, you think better and are certainly better to be around. (See the ''Burnout'' section for more specific ideas.)

COOPERATION TECHNIQUE #2

TO BUILD CONFIDENCE, USE "I WILL . . ."

Both you and your customers benefit when you use the "I will . . ." technique.

1. Your customers will have even more respect for your competence. Many customers feel annoyed when they hear, "I'll try . . ." But they calm down when they hear, "I will." Here is an example. Assume that you are the customer. You are calling to have a new dining table delivered. Imagine how irritated you might feel if you heard, "I will try and have someone there on Thursday, so be sure to be there all day." A much more effective approach would be:

   "I will check with our warehouse about scheduling, and I will call you back before 12:00 today to let you know the exact time and day we can deliver your new dining table."

   Customers like knowing specifically what you will do. They are not left in the dark. "I'll try . . ." is too vague.

   When you tell your customer the actions you will take, you build their confidence in you. It also explains to them why you may not have an immediate answer.

2. You benefit personally by using the "I will . . ." technique. When you say, "I will . . ." and list the steps you will take, you give yourself a head start. You mentally condition yourself to take the needed action. "I will . . ." offers advantages for you—and your customers.

EXERCISE TO DEVELOP YOUR ABILITY

TO BUILD CONFIDENCE USE "I WILL . . ."

HERE ARE SAMPLES TO GET YOU STARTED:

RATHER THAN:	*REPLACE WITH:*
1. "I'll try and get an answer for you from Product Coordination."	"I will call Product Coordination, and I will get back to you before 12:00."
2. "I'll try and transfer your call to Maintenance. You shouldn't have called me."	"I will transfer your call to maintenance. They can answer your question."
3. "Can't you see we're busy? It will take at least half an hour to get that information to you."	"I will get back to you before 4:00."
4. "I'm sorry you had to call back. You know credit people. Nothing makes them hurry."	"I will ______________________ ______________________ ______________________"
5. "Your timing couldn't have been worse. Did you have to call at the end of the day?"	"I will ______________________ ______________________ ______________________"
6. "I'll try and get that information for you today, but it may take me longer."	"I will ______________________ ______________________ ______________________"
7. "I don't know, but I can try."	"I will ______________________ ______________________ ______________________"
8. "I don't know the status of your trouble."	"I will ______________________ ______________________ ______________________"

COOPERATION TECHNIQUE #3

TO REDUCE FRUSTRATION, USE "WILL YOU . . ."

WHY USE THE "WILL YOU . . ." TECHNIQUE? It will help:

- Avoid the irritation that people often feel when they hear "You have to . . ." Those three words make most people bristle. "Will you . . ." is a fast and easy way to get what you want.
- Skip the blaming that "You should have . . ." evokes. A customer is almost automatically going to be defensive when hearing "You should have . . ." "You made a mistake" also carries the stain of blaming.
- Save the confusion people often feel when they don't know specifically what you want. "It would be good to have the report done by Friday," is not as clear as, "Please have the report done by Friday."

WHEN TO USE "WILL YOU . . ."

This handy technique smooths out frustrations. Use "Will you . . ." when:

- You need to communicate in a hurry.
- You did not get what you wanted in the past. For example, you expected a reply to a question last week, but you didn't get it. To reduce that problem you can say, "Will you please have that answer for me before the end of this week?"

If you are not getting what you want and you are also tempted to say, "She should know" or "I shouldn't have to tell her," save yourself and your customer time and frustration. The unexpressed expectation hurts everyone. Ask directly with "Will you . . ."

RATHER THAN:	*REPLACE WITH:*
"You have to . . ." *"You should have . . ."* *"Why didn't you . . ."* *"You made a mistake."* *"I need . . ."*	*"Will you . . ."* *or* *"Will you please . . ."*

USE "WILL YOU. . ." TO REDUCE FRUSTRATION

Will you please circle each statement either: A for Agree
D for Disagree

1. People respond better to, "Will you please complete this job?" than to, "You have to get this job done."	A	D
2. If you say, "Will you please. . .," people will not take you seriously.	A	D
3. If you say, "Will you. . .," people will think you are so nice that they will be calling you all the time, and then you can't get your work done.	A	D
4. Some of the time, "Will you please. . .," works just as well as, "Will you. . ."	A	D
5. "I need the information by Friday," is a statement and the person may or may not tell you if he or she is going to provide the information.	A	D
6. When you ask directly by saying, "Will you. . .," you save everyone's time because people do not need to guess what you are wanting.	A	D
7. The "Will you. . .," technique will not work as well if you use a sarcastic voice tone.	A	D

See author's comments on page 112

TO REDUCE STRESS, USE "WILL YOU . . ."

HERE ARE SAMPLES TO GET YOU STARTED:

RATHER THAN:	*REPLACE WITH:*
1. "You made a mistake."	"Will you double check this number for me."
2. "You should have called earlier."	"Will you call us as soon as you know of any change on the order."
3. "Why didn't you call us when you found out about the changes?"	"Will you call us as soon as you find out about a change? That lead time is so important."

EXERCISE TO DEVELOP YOUR SPEED

TO REDUCE STRESS, USE "WILL YOU . . ."

RATHER THAN:	*REPLACE WITH:*
1. "You have to fill out these forms."	"Will you ____"
2. "I wasn't there when that problem happened. They should have given you the information."	"Will you ____"
3. "You have to call us before Friday."	"Will you ____"
4. "You never give me the data I request."	"Will you ____"
5. "Those two employees are just standing and visiting with each other. They should see how busy I am and help me."	"Will you ____"

COOPERATION TECHNIQUE #4

TO SAY "NO" COURTEOUSLY, USE "YOU CAN . . ."

WHY USE THE "YOU CAN . . ." TECHNIQUE?

- Gain the appreciation of others when you say "no" in a courteous way. Imagine how someone might feel being told, "You can't have it today. You have to wait until tomorrow for the material." A much more courteous expression would be, "You can have the material tomorrow." We respond more favorably to hearing what we *can* do.

  Ninety percent of the people will understand that you are saying "no," but you may run into someone who still says, "I want it today." In such a case, go to Plan B: "I'm sorry. The material is not ready today. It will be ready tomorrow." You will not need to use Plan B very often. Most people catch on the first time.

- Save time by using this technique because you will answer the next question most people will ask: "You said that I can't have it today. Well, when *can* I have it?"

- Make your job easier by saying "You can. . . " Many people find it difficult to say "no" and prefer to find some way to be of assistance. The "You can. . . " approach offers this way of being of service.

WHEN TO USE "YOU CAN . . ."

You will find many opportunities to use this technique in your professional and personal life. Specifically, say "You can . . ." when:

- You cannot provide exactly what your customer is requesting, but you do have an alternative.
- You want to communicate your sincere interest in service even though you may not be able to be of assistance right now.
- Your customer may not know exactly what he or she is requesting. Giving people an option often stimulates their thinking. "No, that's too low of a grade." or "No, that costs too much."

TO SAY "NO" COURTEOUSLY, USE "YOU CAN . . ."

HERE ARE SAMPLES TO GET YOU STARTED:

RATHER THAN:	*REPLACE WITH:*
1. "I don't know anything about that. It's not my job. You have to check with Finance."	"You can get that information from Finance."
2. "You have to request that item in units of 10. We can't get you a single item."	"You can request that item in units of 10."
3. "You can't give us the information over the phone. We can't get it cleared until we have it in writing."	"You can have the document cleared when we receive the information in writing."

EXERCISE TO DEVELOP YOUR SPEED

TO SAY "NO" COURTEOUSLY, USE "YOU CAN . . ."

RATHER THAN:	*REPLACE WITH:*
1. "We don't have that data. You have to call Central Services."	"You can ________________________________ ________________________________"
2. "There's nothing I can do. You have to talk with a manager."	"You can ________________________________ ________________________________"
3. "That's not our responsibility. You have to get that taken care of by your local organization."	"You can ________________________________ ________________________________"
4. "You have to give us two days notice to have that kind of job done."	"You can ________________________________ ________________________________"
5. "We won't have the quality of material you want in stock until next week. We only have a lower quality available today."	"You can ________________________________ ________________________________"

COOPERATION TECHNIQUE #5

TO SAVE TIME, GIVE THE REASON FIRST

WHY USE THE TECHNIQUE OF GIVE THE REASON FIRST?

- The human mind is created with the desire to know why. Think how often a growing child asks, ''Why?'' When someone is providing information, the question that is darting through most people's minds and taking most of their concentration is ''Why?'' Capitalize on that reality. Give the reason first.

- You get people's attention more rapidly when you explain the reason first. For example: ''To save you money. . .'' or ''Here is the answer to your question.''

WHEN TO USE THE TECHNIQUE OF ''GIVE THE REASON FIRST''

- When you are communicating technical information that the other person may not understand.

- When you think the other person may not cooperate.

- When the other person may not know you or may not trust your experience.

USE THE OTHER PERSON'S REASON

You get even more cooperation when you express how your message will benefit your customer. Here are some examples:

''To help save you time. . .''

''To help me complete your request more rapidly. . .''

''So that I can access your records. . .''

TO SAVE TIME, GIVE THE REASON FIRST

HERE ARE SAMPLES TO GET YOU STARTED:

RATHER THAN:	*REPLACE WITH:*
1. ''You have to use one of our service facilities. It keeps your costs down.''	''To keep your costs down, will you use our service facilities?''
2. ''I can't see if a final adjustment has been issued without your job number.''	''So that I can check and see if your final adjustment has been issued, will you please give me your job number?''
3. ''Why can't you get your processing done on time? I can't call the client with an answer until you give me this information.''	''The client is eager for this information. Will you give me this answer?''

EXERCISE TO DEVELOP YOUR SPEED

TO SAVE TIME, GIVE THE REASON FIRST

RATHER THAN:	*REPLACE WITH:*
1. "I can't get those summaries completed because your handwriting is too sloppy. You have to print it so I can read it."	______________________
2. "You should have sent the document. We can't process your renewal without it."	______________________
3. "We can't give you your new identification number on the phone. We have to mail it to you. We have to protect your account."	______________________
4. "Can't you see I'm busy with a rush project? I can't do your report until this afternoon."	______________________
5. "I can't give you a status report right now. I need to isolate the trouble first."	______________________

COOPERATION TECHNIQUE #6

TO REDUCE TENSION, CALL ANYWAY

Isn't it amazing how much customers will accept if you keep them informed of the progress? If you do not let people know what is happening, and then surprise them with a delay, there will probably be trouble. When you anticipate and keep people informed about a potential delay, they are much more cooperative.

You benefit also. Nothing is quite so draining as knowing that you have negative news to tell someone, gritting your teeth when the telephone rings, and hoping it isn't that person on the line. When you call anyway, you take control. You call when you are ready rather than waiting until your customer has erupted into a volcano and is calling you.

Call anyway. You reduce your feelings of tension and you build your customer's trust in you.

Use the following discussion questions to sharpen your skill in this problem-preventing approach.

CALL ANYWAY

1. When you have negative news to tell someone, how does this affect your concentration? And how do you feel whenever the telephone rings?

____

____

____

2. How does it waste your time when you wait and don't call with negative news?

____

____

____

3. What are specific techniques you can use to get yourself to call anyway?

____

____

____

4. Why do people appreciate knowing negative news rather than not hearing anything?

____

____

____

RECAP
SECTION TECHNIQUES

To get the most out of this section, check the techniques you will benefit by using more frequently.

I will:

- ☐ Use a warm and cooperative voice tone . . . *to reduce hostility*
- ☐ Use "I will . . ." *to build confidence*
- ☐ Use "Will you . . ." *to reduce frustration*
- ☐ Use "You can . . ." *to say "no" courteously*
- ☐ Give the reason first . . . *to save time*
- ☐ Call anyway . . . *to reduce stress*
- ☐ Say specifically what I have done, or will do . . . *to show sincerity*

Benefits come with practice. If you are using a technique 75% of the time, move it up to 100%. Make your job easier by making it easier for people to do what you want. Remember, practice makes permanent.

FOR REINFORCEMENT
SAY TO YOURSELF:

"I make it easy for people to cooperate with me. I search for and incorporate good techniques which can be tailored to fit my personality and the situation. I have less frustration because I use the techniques every opportunity."

Now that you have some specific tools in hand, what overall system will help you use the tools on a continuing basis? The answer is ongoing customer feedback, and that is what the next section explores.

PART IV

MAINTAINING CUSTOMER SATISFACTION

SECTION EIGHT

BUILDING MOTIVATION WITH CUSTOMER FEEDBACK

PREVIEW

The biggest reason that people do not provide quality customer satisfaction is:

They do not have adequate information about when they are and are not satisfying customers.

The cure is feedback.

BUILDING MOTIVATION WITH CUSTOMER FEEDBACK

''Hey, hey, hey! We met goal at 3:30 today.''

The kind of energy the above statement conveys will not come through any amount of ''attaboy's'' or ''attagirls.'' Employee benefits will not produce it. Good supervision is not enough. Good people are not enough. Even the techniques for getting cooperation are not enough.

To sustain a high level of motivation, we all need feedback about how well we are achieving our targets.

THE MISSING INGREDIENT

Abraham Maslow, the famous psychologist, pointed out that satisfied needs are not motivators. It's true. We are motivated more by what we are missing. Targets give us something to miss. Feedback lets us know how we are doing.

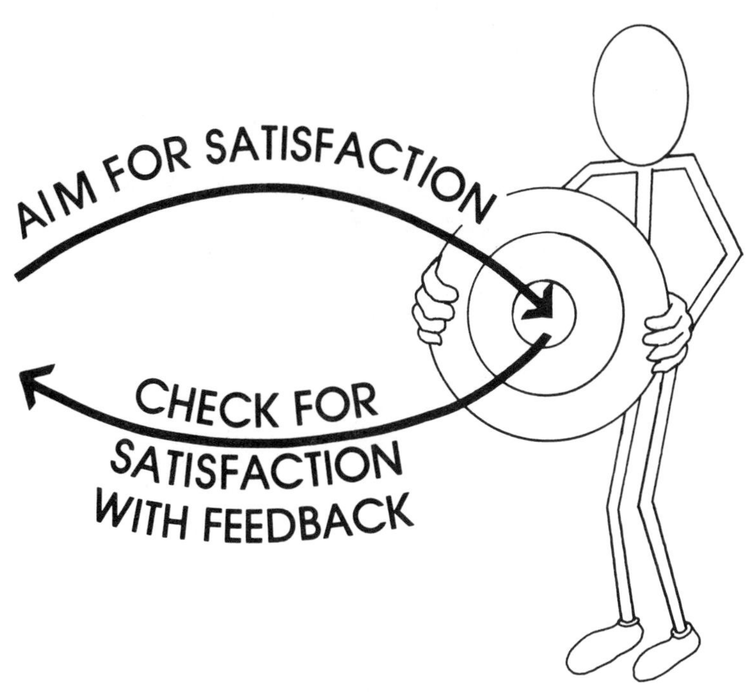

CHECK FOR CUSTOMER SATISFACTION

Give yourself a head start with these personal benefits by checking with your customers for satisfaction.

Place a check mark by the one that is *most* important to you. I plan to:

- ☐ Reduce stress by having a focus that is energizing and motivating.
- ☐ Save time by avoiding having to do things that my customer does not really want.
- ☐ Enjoy more satisfaction by learning to skip ''How am I doing?'' concerns. When you check with customers for satisfaction, you know how you are doing.

Someone might say, *''I know I do good work because I've done it for years.''* But this individual never really knows how good his or her work is until there is a check for satisfaction with the customer.

You might hear, *''Oh, I know they're satisfied. If they aren't, they always complain.''* Again, the provider really does not know. Some people will complain to dozens of others without ever telling the organization that provided the product or service.

Another dangerous comment is *''I know what they want.''* This approach often causes problems because a customer receives a product or service that is not what was expected.

WHAT HAS HAPPENED TO YOU?

Think of some situations in your professional or personal life where you were the customer. Pick one where the service was not up to your expectations and the person providing the service did not bother checking with you to see how satisfied you were. Write your responses in the space provided.

Situation where you were the customer and you did not get what you wanted:

____

____

____

____

____

How did you feel and what did you do later?

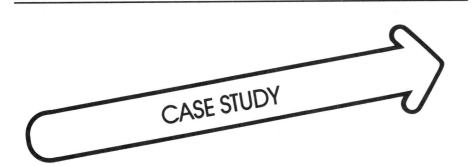

____

____

____

____

____

CASE STUDY

CASE STUDY
GREG AND CUSTOMER FEEDBACK

Chris, a carpenter, was overheard to say: ''I always knew that we were supposed to do the best job possible, and it never bothered me if I had to go back and forth to the job site two or three times before completing the repair.

''Then our team started getting feedback on requests we handled. Our clients were asked, 'Was the job completed on the first visit?' The answer was usually, 'No.'

''My boss had told me to complete everything in the first trip (one trip), but I didn't think it was that important. I only recognized how important it was when our department starting putting 'job completed first visit' on the customer feedback form.

''Although we thought we were doing a good job, our customers reported they wanted the repair work completed the first trip. Now I call the person making the request before I go. With a list of questions, I find out what tools and materials we need to take. It has made the job easier. And with customer feedback my boss spends less time telling me things.''

Customer feedback makes the job easier!

A PRACTICAL SYSTEM FOR OBTAINING FEEDBACK

Asking for feedback will help you get your priorities into focus. But it's not always easy to get feedback from your customers—even from those with whom you work most closely. They may think that you should automatically know how they feel about your service. Or, they may dislike giving any negative feedback that "might hurt your feelings." Often the fear of hurting someone's feelings ends up in wasting time because important information is not communicated and in the end hurt feelings happen anyway.

A streamlined way to obtain feedback that can be tailored and used by anyone is explained in *The Art of Communicating* by Bert Decker which can be ordered using the information in the back of this book. The system quickly and courteously teaches a reader how to obtain valuable feedback.

THREE PLUSES AND THREE MINUSES

One approach to obtain feedback is to tell a customer:

"I want to make sure my work is satisfying your expectations. Will you tell me three things you like about my work? And three things we need to do to improve our service?"

By asking for the pluses first, you encourage people to get those valuable minuses on the table where you can deal with them.

Sometimes people hesitate asking for feedback because they believe that if they asked, the customer will not stop spilling out complaints and demands. This rarely happens. Most people are pleased to be asked, and their comments are moderate and helpful.

PROTECT YOURSELF WITH ONGOING FEEDBACK

Ongoing feedback will build a productive foundation for you. If you depend on only complaints and compliments, you are on shaky footing. Here's why. Robbed of ongoing feedback, the complaint triples in impact. One complaint can cloud all the good work you have accomplished in previous transactions with a customer. By requesting regular feedback, you will not only earn the respect of your customer, you will also begin to hear positive comments about how your service has improved.

GET ONGOING CUSTOMER FEEDBACK

It is easy to lull yourself into a false security if you don't get ongoing feedback from customers. What are some practical ways that work groups can get input from the people they serve?

- Why is systematic feedback important?
- What are some examples of feedback systems that work well?

The questionnaire on the next page will help you formulate ideas for a systematic feedback mechanism.

SAMPLE QUESTIONNAIRE

GET ONGOING FEEDBACK FROM YOUR CUSTOMERS

Here are some ideas to stimulate your thinking. What questions would be the most useful to ask the people your work group serves?

1. How well do we keep you informed of the status of work we are doing for you?

Not at all	*Somewhat*	*Usually*	*To a large degree*	*Completely*
________	________	________	________	________

2. How often do we meet agreed-up deadlines?

Never	*Rarely*	*Usually*	*Most of the time*	*Always*
________	________	________	________	________

3. How do you rate the quality of work we complete for you?

Unsatisfactory	*Poor*	*Acceptable*	*Good*	*Excellent*
________	________	________	________	________

4. How well do we check back with you to make sure we have completed the work?

Not at all	*Somewhat*	*Usually*	*To a large degree*	*Completely*
________	________	________	________	________

5. How would you describe the cost of services we provide you?

Too Expensive	*Somewhat Expensive*	*Acceptable*	*Good Value*	*Excellent Value*
________	________	________	________	________

6. How well do we communicate that we want to serve you?

Not at all	*Somewhat*	*Usually*	*To a large degree*	*Very well*
________	________	________	________	________

7. Other comments ____

____

____

____

THE BEST KIND OF CUSTOMER FEEDBACK

You save the most time and build the best teamwork when you have feedback that is:

- Ongoing
- Specific
- Centered on the end-use customer
- Focused on a limited number of vital indicators
- Available on a timely basis
- Available to all key people in the organization regardless of level
- Portrayed on a line graph. When the desired results are achieved, the line goes up.

Why are these feedback features so important? What problems do they prevent?

____

____

____

CONSIDER YOUR OWN RESPONSIBILITIES

Can you provide the name or job title of five people for whom you provide work or a service? When did you last check with each to see how well you are satisfying his or her expectations?

	Name	Most Recent Feedback Date
1.	______________________	__________
2.	______________________	__________
3.	______________________	__________
4.	______________________	__________
5.	______________________	__________

TALK ABOUT CUSTOMER FEEDBACK

To get the most value from feedback, follow these three guides:

Talk successes

Talk specifics

Talk daily

Since feedback is such an important means of motivation, make some notes in the space provided and discuss your comments with your manager.

1. Considering that our work can be problem solving oriented, why is it important to talk about successes in customer satisfaction? ____________________

 ____

2. When we receive feedback that our work has satisfied customers, it is easy to ignore it. Why is it so easy to disregard positive feedback? ____________________

 ____

3. An ''Atta boy'' rarely works. It sounds insincere. On the other hand, discussing specifics will communicate. This is particularly important when talking about positive customer feedback. What are some examples of specific, positive customer feedback that you have given or received during the last month? ____________________

 ____

4. Talking about customer feedback each day keeps customer satisfaction in focus. What systems and habits can you use to make sure you talk about customer feedback each day? ____________________

 ____

RECAP
SECTION TECHNIQUES

To get the most out of this chapter, check the techniques you will benefit by using more frequently.

I will:

- ☐ Add meaning to my work by getting feedback from the people I serve.
- ☐ Develop a system to encourage ongoing feedback.

FOR REINFORCEMENT
SAY TO YOURSELF:

"I go out of my way to get feedback from my customers. It makes my job easier and it keeps me going strong."

As you wrap up the last section in the book, the final question is how to put the ideas you have learned into action. The final few pages will pull together some practical ways to reduce stress, get more done, and insure you achieve customer satisfaction — the other half of your job.

PART V

EPILOGUE

EPILOGUE

Winston Churchill left us with a legacy of leadership and inspiration that applies to many situations—including customer satisfaction. Churchill affirmed, *"Never, never, never give up."*

This is especially true with customer satisfaction. Developing the skills and getting the results you want require ongoing reinforcement. Habits that hurt customer satisfaction may have been developed over a lifetime. New habits can replace the old ones only by practicing the new behavior over and over until it feels natural.

CONCENTRATE ON YOUR RESPONSIBILITIES

Be selective in your reinforcements. As you read this book the first time, pick the techniques that have special value for your responsibilities and your personality. You can review this book again later. At that time, select a different set of techniques to convert to habits.

A GREAT PLACE TO START

If this book has caused you to begin to concentrate on the second half of your job, great! One way to succeed is to consider the main technique in each section. Fifteen years of work enhancing customer satisfaction validate the impact of the seven tools previously taught. To review, these techniques are:

- **TAKE THINGS PROFESSIONALLY AND NOT PERSONALLY.**
- **SPOT BURNOUT EARLY AND PREVENT IT.**
- **TREAT EACH PERSON AS A CUSTOMER TO GET MORE COOPERATION.**
- **AIM FOR CUSTOMER SATISFACTION, NOT JUST SERVICE.**
- **SOLVE PROBLEMS WITHOUT BLAMING YOURSELF OR OTHERS.**
- **PRACTICE PROVEN TECHNIQUES.**
- **ENCOURAGE ONGOING FEEDBACK.**

IN CONCLUSION

WHY FIVE?

As you read on page 7 of the book, don't attempt to do everything this book recommends at once. Instead, concentrate on up to five techniques. Select those that are most appropriate from the buffet of ideas presented. If you pick 20 techniques, it is easy to put them aside and wait for the elusive day of "when I have more time." By focusing your selection, it is easier to keep yourself moving forward.

MAKE THE SELECTION EASY

Review the recap page of each section. Notice which techniques you checked. Use these as a starting point to select those most important to you.

FOR YOUR CONVENIENCE

To make it easier to choose your techniques, here are the page numbers for each of the recaps.

YOUR PERSONAL ACTION PLAN

YOUR PERSONAL CUSTOMER SATISFACTION ACTION PLAN

WHAT ARE THE CUSTOMER SATISFACTION TECHNIQUES YOU HAVE SELECTED TO BEGIN WORKING ON? LIST THEM IN THE SPACE PROVIDED

1. ____

2. ____

3. ____

4. ____

5. ____

A FINAL WORD

Build in time to work on customer satisfaction techniques during the next thirty days. Build your skill in each technique by using some of the following suggestions:

YOUR CALENDAR

Write one of the techniques you selected on your calendar for today. Write a second on the "tomorrow" page. Note one technique each day for the next month. As you refer to your calendar during the course of work, take some time to practice the technique listed for that day.

CARDS

An alternative to the calendar idea is to write each technique on a separate card. Place each card in a conspicuous (but different) place in your work area. Practice each new technique until it becomes a habit.

THE COMPLETE LIST

Post the complete listing of your techniques near the phone. Look at it whenever you are on hold. Use this "waiting" time to reinforce yourself.

NOTICE YOUR SUCCESSES

When you use your techniques and get better results, compliment yourself. Talk about your successes with supportive coworkers and your boss.

WORK AS A TEAM

Ask a coworker to read *Customer Satisfaction: The Other Half of Your Job* and talk together about what was covered in each section. Discuss your mutual development plans. Give each other encouragement to head in the right direction.

SOME FRINGE BENEFITS

As you enhance your ability to handle the second half of your job, the people part, you will enjoy some attractive fringe benefits. Your personal relationships will improve. Even though this book concentrates on job issues, the techniques presented will enrich your personal life. "Will you . . ." helps relationships articulate unexpressed expectations. Giving a reason first takes the sting out of negative feedback. Taking it professionally and not personally helps calm conflict.

Enjoy these fringe benefits. Enjoy the people part of your job. Enjoy the confidence that comes from accepting the challenge of the other half of your job.

YOUR FEEDBACK IS IMPORTANT

This book is the result of feedback from hundreds of people in research groups and seminars. Feedback is vital to be of continuing value. For this reason, please take a moment and note three pluses and three minuses for you in reading this book. You are welcome to use this sheet. Thank you for your ideas.

+ ____

+ ____

+ ____

– ____

– ____

– ____

Please mail to: DRU SCOTT
CUSTOMER SATISFACTION TOOLS
c/o CRISP PUBLICATIONS, INC.
1200 Hamilton Court
Menlo Park, California 94025

AUTHOR RESPONSES

SECTION FOUR—PAGE 43
"BUT I DON'T HAVE CUSTOMERS" AGREE/DISAGREE EXERCISE
1-D; 2-A; 3-D; 4-D; 5-D; 6-D; 7-D; 8-A; 9-A

SECTION FIVE—PAGE 55
AIM FOR SATISFACTION
1-A; 2-D; 3-D; 4-A; 5-A; 6-A; 7-A; 8-A; 9-A

SECTION SIX—PAGE 61
BELIEFS AS A BARRIER TO PROBLEM SOLVING
1-D; 2-D; 3-D; 4-D; 5-D; 6-A; 7-D; 8-D; 9-A; 10-D

SECTION SEVEN—PAGE 83
USE "WILL YOU..." TO REDUCE FRUSTRATION
1-A; 2-D; 3-D; 4-A, 5-A, 6-A, 7-A

NOTES

FOR OTHER FIFTY-MINUTE SELF-STUDY BOOKS
SEE THE BACK OF THIS BOOK.

NOTES

FOR OTHER FIFTY-MINUTE SELF-STUDY BOOKS
SEE THE BACK OF THIS BOOK.

NOTES

FOR OTHER FIFTY-MINUTE SELF-STUDY BOOKS
SEE THE BACK OF THIS BOOK.

NOTES

FOR OTHER FIFTY-MINUTE SELF-STUDY BOOKS
SEE THE BACK OF THIS BOOK.

NOTES

FOR OTHER FIFTY-MINUTE SELF-STUDY BOOKS
SEE THE BACK OF THIS BOOK.

NOTES

NOTES

FOR OTHER FIFTY-MINUTE SELF-STUDY BOOKS
SEE THE BACK OF THIS BOOK.

NOTES

FOR OTHER FIFTY-MINUTE SELF-STUDY BOOKS
SEE THE BACK OF THIS BOOK.

OVER 150 BOOKS AND 35 VIDEOS AVAILABLE IN THE 50-MINUTE SERIES

50-Minute Series Books and Videos Subject Areas . . .

Management
Training
Human Resources
Customer Service and Sales Training
Communications
Small Business and Financial Planning
Creativity
Personal Development
Wellness
Adult Literacy and Learning
Career, Retirement and Life Planning

Other titles available from Crisp Publications in these categories

Crisp Computer Series
The Crisp Small Business & Entrepreneurship Series
Quick Read Series
Management
Personal Development
Retirement Planning